D0481273

PRAISE FOR *AN OUTLAW AND A LADY*

"Jessi's words offer a tale of hope, faith, persistence, and strength. . . . No matter the storm or travail, Jessi has remained true to her heart and on course."

—JOHN CARTER CASH

"Jessi Colter Jennings—the tiniest, most compact version of real spiritual power on earth that I've ever known—has told a story so true to the bone that I am more in awe of her now than ever. She has guided me with invincible conviction when I could have thrown her over my shoulder in a heartbeat. Her love never fails. Her faith puts you on your heels. You just don't mess with Jessi. Her autobiography tells you the how and why of one of life's greatest love stories, and I can imagine Waylon's twinkling eyes throughout."

—LISA KRISTOFFERSON

"Jessi's autobiography describes the best years of our lives with the Highwaymen and makes me sad that the road didn't go on forever and the party did end. Jessi's narrative of her life with Waylon through good times and bad is an example of a life well-led. Loving and letting go and without regret. Waylon was a very lucky man. Jessi continues to love and inspire humanity, and I count myself blessed to be her friend."

—KRIS KRISTOFFERSON

"Waylon Jennings was a great talent, a good friend of mine, and one of the greatest pickers and singers ever. Jessi Colter is one of my favorite singers— always has been. I love her for being a great friend and partner to Waylon, one who stayed with him through thick and thin."

—WILLIE NELSON

"Jessi Colter was a seminal figure in one of twentieth-century America's most profound cultural shifts: the Outlaw Country Movement. Her vivid account brings the era back to life with a unique perspective. It's a compelling tale told by one of the most soulful women on Earth."

—DON WAS, RECORD PRODUCER, MUSICIAN, AND PRESIDENT OF BLUE NOTE RECORDS

"As the only female on the now infamous *Wanted: The Outlaws* album, Jessi Colter was and is still the First Lady of Outlaw Music and her memoir reflects the many trials and tribulations that came along with that role. Her book is packed with stories of family, friends, and faith (and the lack thereof). Clearly it wasn't easy, and it was never dull."

—JAMEY JOHNSON, SINGER-SONGWRITER

"Jessi Colter sings, and now writes, with a light that illuminates this beautiful and moving inspirational tale of love, faith, and belief in the healing power of song."

—LENNY KAYE, GUITARIST, COAUTHOR OF *WAYLON*

"If the art of living is the ability to use faith, courage, loyalty, and sacrifice, Jessie Colter, in this beautiful book—a love story and a joy to read—has provided a wonderful example of how each of these traits is to be accomplished. It transcends storytelling and becomes an inspiration. It is a book we treasure, as you will too, from a woman every bit as beautiful as the prose she writes. Her life's devotion to Waylon stands as a monument to her character."

—JAY AND REMA GOLDBERG

"Jessi's words jump off the pages like the lyrics of a great song jump into your heart. She's not Lisa; she will always be Waylon's Angel."

—CARL P. MAYFIELD, NASHVILLE-BASED, NATIONALLY SYNDICATED RADIO PERSONALITY AND MEMBER OF THE RADIO HALL OF FAME

An Outlaw and a Lady

A MEMOIR OF MUSIC, LIFE WITH WAYLON,
AND THE FAITH THAT BROUGHT ME HOME

JESSI COLTER

WITH DAVID RITZ

NELSON
BOOKS

An Imprint of Thomas Nelson

© 2017 by Mirriam Jennings

All rights reserved. No portion of this book may be reproduced, stored in a retrieval system, or transmitted in any form or by any means—electronic, mechanical, photocopy, recording, scanning, or other—except for brief quotations in critical reviews or articles, without the prior written permission of the publisher.

Published in Nashville, Tennessee, by Nelson Books, an imprint of Thomas Nelson. Nelson Books and Thomas Nelson are registered trademarks of HarperCollins Christian Publishing, Inc.

Thomas Nelson titles may be purchased in bulk for educational, business, fund-raising, or sales promotional use. For information, please e-mail SpecialMarkets@ThomasNelson.com.

Any Internet addresses, phone numbers, or company or product information printed in this book are offered as a resource and are not intended in any way to be or to imply an endorsement by Thomas Nelson, nor does Thomas Nelson vouch for the existence, content, or services of these sites, phone numbers, companies, or products beyond the life of this book.

Unless otherwise noted, Scripture quotations are taken from the New King James Version˚. © 1982 by Thomas Nelson. Used by permission. All rights reserved.

Scripture quotations marked KJV are taken from the King James Version. Public domain.

ISBN 978–0718082987 (eBook)

Library of Congress Cataloging-in-Publication Data
Names: Colter, Jessi. | Ritz, David.
Title: An outlaw and a lady : a memoir of music, life with Waylon, and the faith that brought me home / Jessi Colter with David Ritz.
Description: Nashville, Tennessee : Nelson Books, [2017] | Includes bibliographical references.
Identifiers: LCCN 2016035030 | ISBN 9780718082970
Subjects: LCSH: Colter, Jessi. | Country musicians--United States--Biography. | Christian biography--United States. | Jennings, Waylon.
Classification: LCC ML420.C654 A3 2017 | DDC 782.421642092 [B] --dc23 LC record available at https://lccn.loc.gov/2016035030

Printed in the United States of America

17 18 19 20 21   LSC   10 9 8 7 6 5 4 3 2 1

For Waylon

CONTENTS

CONTENTS

INTRODUCTION

I NEVER IMAGINED WRITING A BOOK ABOUT MYSELF. IT WASN'T that I was unaware of leading an adventurous and exciting life. Adventure and excitement have been there since childhood. I've been privileged to be part of a cast of amazing characters—everyone from Johnny Cash to George Jones to Willie Nelson and Kris Kristofferson— larger-than-life individuals of wondrous charm, humor, intelligence, and spirit. But, until now, I lacked that certain something that allowed me to say, "I've got a story I need to tell."

Maybe that's because for thirty-three years I was married to Waylon Jennings, whose story overwhelmed nearly everyone around him. I don't say that begrudgingly. I say it lovingly. Those were the best thirty-three years of my life, a time when I was more than happy to allow Waylon to take the lead as chief storyteller. When it came to telling stories, Waylon was a master. In 1996, six years before crossing over to the other side of time, Waylon wrote his autobiography (with our dear friend Lenny Kaye), a fully realized portrait that captures all his energy and honesty. I was convinced that book, dedicated to me, relayed everything that needed to be said about Waylon and our loving relationship. My ego—such as it is—required no more attention.

But then things began shifting when I received a call from David Ritz, who, having recently completed working on Willie Nelson's autobiography, *It's a Long Story*, called to interview me for a television tribute he was writing about Waylon. As a Jewish convert to Christianity, David expressed interest in the story of my faith.

My faith.

Those two words touched me. The more pointed the questions David posed, the more I saw the possibility—even the joy—of tracing the evolution of my relationship with God. Rather than use the occasion to trumpet my accomplishments, what about a narrative that traced God's accomplishments in my life? Since I owe it all to God—my breath, my soul, my every last experience on earth—why not view the writing process as a way to give God the glory?

Part of what drew David to my story was something I said early in our conversation: that for many years—critical years when I was young and especially impressionable—I had lost my faith. And I lost it in spite of being raised by the most faithful mother imaginable: a woman who served God as a charismatic evangelist.

"You found faith early," said David, "then lost it, only to regain it under the most unlikely circumstances. That's heavy drama."

When he put it that way, I began to see the shape of a story that is as spiritual as it is musical. I began to feel the need to tell it. I began to understand that my faith journey need not be an exercise in ego, but more a prayer.

I pray simply that my experiences—especially those long, exciting, and challenging times with Waylon—come alive and touch the hearts of everyone reading this book.

--- Part One ---

THE CLOUD

Chapter 1

ARIZONA AT NIGHT

Sara Teasdale, an American poet, wrote some lines of haunting verse in 1915, a generation before my parents left Indiana at the beginning of the Great Depression and headed west, thus marking the start of the bold adventure that has led to this history of my heart.

The moon is a charring ember
Dying into the dark;
Off in the crouching mountains
Coyotes bark.

The stars are heavy in heaven,
Too great for the sky to hold—
What if they fell and shattered
The earth with gold?

No lights are over the mesa,
The wind is hard and wild,
I stand at the darkened window
And cry like a child.[1]

I invoke the poet's heart because she sets the stage so beautifully. The stark and breathtaking landscape of Arizona is the essential backdrop to this story. It is where I was born Mirriam Rebecca Joan Johnson on May 25, 1943. It is where I reside today. It is where all the essential discoveries of my life have taken place—the discovery of my faith, the discovery of my ability to make music, and the discovery of both my husbands.

For me, Arizona is a magical land whose mysteries are as ancient as they are beautiful. The deserts. The mountains. The rocks. The sky. The myths. The stories of the Native Americans, the cowboys, the explorers, the miners, the pioneers. The spirit driving these stories is the same spirit that drove my father, Arnold Hobson Johnson, and my mother, Helen D. Perkins Johnson, to this untamed and primitive land.

Drive is the right word because Daddy, a man of many mechanical talents, was a professional race-car driver. Born in 1898 and raised in Linton, Indiana, just outside Indianapolis, as a young man he competed against Louis Chevrolet and the Dodge Brothers, winning prize money all over the Midwest. More than a driver, he was also a designer who could build cars by himself from the ground up. He possessed scientific genius and an active mind that sought to solve geological and metallurgical puzzles of the highest order. His lifelong passion was mining.

Before marrying Arnold Johnson and heading west, Helen Perkins had established a boardinghouse and worked as a cosmetologist in Indiana. She had been born in Green County, Kentucky, where her father, a coal miner, had raised his six daughters as a single dad. His wife—my maternal grandmother—died when Mother was three years old. Four years younger than Arnold, Helen was a professional woman at a time when, especially in the Midwest, that was a rarity. She married Arnold and willingly went with him to Arizona, not only because she had fallen in love with his romantic spirit, but because two of her sisters were already living there.

They first came to Tempe where Dad opened a garage. Car repair was as good a Depression-proof job as any—and Dad was a whiz at it. He and Mother fell in love with the land. There were outdoor parties down by the river in a brush arbor on Saturday evenings where Mother loved to dance the night away. The world was simple and pleasant. The future held promise. But then tragedy stuck. My mother contracted tuberculosis. And then, without warning, my father, who loved his cigars, was diagnosed with throat cancer.

Panic set in. Doctors were consulted, but doctors in that rural community were in short supply. Remedies were prescribed, yet the predictions were dire. The family was told that both diseases would eventually prove fatal. Even at its very beginning, their new life seemed over.

Then came a knock on the door. It was late at night. I imagine a night like the one described in Sara Teasdale's poem. "No lights are over the mesa, the wind is hard and wild, I stand at the darkened window and cry like a child."

I imagine my mother crying, questioning the cruelty of fate that would allow her to embark on this great western adventure, only to see it turn deadly.

I imagine her wiping away her tears and answering the door. Two men appeared.

"We have been sent," they said simply.

"By whom?" she asked.

"By God," they answered.

"For what reason?"

"To pray. We have come to pray for healing."

Until this moment, my parents had never been overtly religious. Dad was an engineer, designer, and scientist. Mother was a businesswoman. But something prompted them to invite these strangers into their home. They allowed these two men to lay hands on them. They held hands and prayed. They prayed out loud and they prayed in silence. I can't tell you what went on in the minds of my mother and father as the two men covered them in prayer. I don't know the degree of their skepticism or doubt. All I know is that they were willing. They submitted. They allowed. They were slain in the Spirit. And then they saw the results.

Over a period of weeks, Mother saw that all the signs of tuberculosis had dissipated. When my father returned to the hospital in Phoenix, his doctor was in disbelief.

"The cancer is gone," he said. "It is in total remission. I can't explain it."

"I can," said Mother, who was by Daddy's side. "I can explain it in a word."

"Please do," urged the physician.

"God. The wonders and miracles of God."

From that day forward, Mother was a changed woman. She devoted her life not only to the study of God's Word but to its application in the lives of others. She became an apostle, a pentecostal preacher whose passion for Christ and his healing ministry never waned. She didn't simply read the New Testament; she lived it. Her fervor for God was matched only by her compassion. And her energy, fueled by her faith, was inexhaustible.

Father's energy matched Mother's. While he never tried to subdue her spiritual exuberance—that would have been impossible—his own passion moved in an entirely different direction. He arrived in the Wild West at precisely that moment when mining fever was sweeping the land. Dad caught that fever. He met an old-time prospector by the name of Lloyd Serick, who took him to a spot in the Arizona wilderness that Dad purchased: the Rare Metals Mine. The mine's primary metal was molybdenum. And in 1942, as part of the war effort, my father obtained a loan from the US government to mine molybdenum, an alloy in the hardening of steel. Dad never got rich mining, but mining was never about money for him. It was about the indefatigable pursuit of discovery. As a committed miner, he couldn't be stopped.

Born during World War II, I was my parent's sixth child after Mary Delores, Helen Lucille, David, Paul, and Sharon, who was only two years my senior. John, the baby, was born two years after me. Because Mary, Helen, and David were much older and had moved out of the house, my closest siblings were Paul, Sharon, and John.

The central setting of my childhood was Mesa, a Mormon city some twenty miles east of Phoenix. And within that setting the central image was a large, white neon sign in the shape of a lighthouse that towered over our residence, a converted army barracks. The sign, lit day and night, said "Lighthouse Mission." The official name of Mother's church was First Lighthouse Evangelical Center.

Mesa was a small city where real estate was inexpensive. As industrious as they were practical, my parents were able to buy this abandoned barracks for very little. A sanctuary accommodating some sixty worshippers stood on one side; our living quarters were on the other. The result was an organic feeling of natural unity: we lived where we worshipped and worshipped where we lived.

Two seminal passions informed my upbringing: my mother's passion for Jesus and my dad's passion for mining. The two were never in conflict. In fact, they complemented each other. My mother encouraged my father's mining efforts just as my father supported my mother's ministry. These two adults, whose influence on me is incalculable, were all about adventure—Mother adventurously sought God's eternal truths; Daddy adventurously sought minerals hidden deep beneath the soil.

My folks were unique individuals preoccupied with what some might consider esoteric matters, yet they were down-to-earth, here-and-now parents constitutionally incapable of ignoring their children. I never wanted for attention. I saw Daddy as a quiet man, a studious soul who, after spending hours absorbing a complex chemistry text, could get up, go out and build fences, repair tractors, and then put on a coat and tie to sell bankers shares in his Century Molybdenum Copper Corporation—all in a day's work.

Mother's energy took a different turn. She was more intense. Because God had given her all the gifts of the Spirit, including healing, she felt compelled to use those gifts—and use them extravagantly. She also felt compelled to make me understand that before I was born she had heard God speak my name—Mirriam—and a prophecy was given that I would serve him in a special way.

Mother's absolute conviction was that we stood in the heritage of the saints and in the bloodline of Christ Jesus. From infancy on, I watched and heard her preach with piercing eloquence about the grandeur of God's healing love. Miracles and wonders surrounded my childhood. I bore witness to a dead baby brought back to life. I saw palsied men cured before my very eyes. As a child, I experienced dramatic firsthand evidence of God's goodness, mercy, and grace.

And then I experienced something else: music. There was an upright piano in the sanctuary that drew me like a magnet. I was fascinated by the sounds made by those white and black keys. At an early age I could pick out little melodies. When Mother saw my interest, she made certain that I had piano lessons. I also learned accordion.

All this music, of course, was linked to the love I was feeling in Mother's church. She could preach, but I soon learned that I could sing. All this came about without effort. The process of channeling music through my heart was—and remains—a natural one. It was clearly a gift. I cannot remember an instance when music ever perplexed or frustrated me. If I heard it in my head, I could play it or sing it.

I understand that for some making music can be a struggle, but for me, beginning in childhood, music flowed like a clear mountain stream whose source, I learned from Mother, was God on high. Music would prove to be the great instrument of change in my life, the ethereal spirit that would, in one form or another, punctuate my story with one surprise after another.

Chapter 2

WHEN TIME AND ETERNITY MEET

As an adult, I discovered the following beautiful words by C. S. Lewis: "For the Present is the point at which time touches eternity. Of the present moment, and of it only, humans have an experience analogous to the experience which God has of reality as a whole."[1] Yet the moment of which he speaks—the moment of experiencing eternal time—happened when I was a child. I didn't understand the underpinning theology, and I didn't have to. I processed the phenomenon as pure joy. It was a moment when, in the midst of Sunday services at Mother's church, I sang a very old hymn whose title echoes the same sentiment as C. S. Lewis's words:

When Time and Eternity Meet

I sat on the banks of a river
I stood on the crest of a hill
I gazed at the great modern cities
The valleys serene and so still.
I heard the loud roar of the ocean,
I felt the great desert's heat.
Then I thought of the fate of this whole wide world
Where time and eternity meet.[2]

Though music is rooted in time, music took me out of time. It suspended time. Playing and singing music gave me a feeling of freedom. Music made sense to me. Its meters made mathematical sense. I didn't have to count out the bars and the beats. I felt them. They fell together in a rhythm as natural as the beats of my heart. And the most beautiful thing about my first music—this beatific music of my childhood—was its message. The purpose was praise. And the praise was other-directed and otherworldly. The praise was for God and God alone.

When my musical ability was praised by Mother and her congregants, that felt good—but not nearly as good as worshipping the goodness of God in song. As a performer, I never felt especially gifted. I was grateful to be able to play and sing, but I took it in stride. I realized I had talent, although that talent never went to my head. If there was a gift that impressed me, it was not my own. It was Mother's. Her gift—to reflect the sweet compassion of Christ in word and deed—overwhelmed my world. I followed her every thought, watched her every move, mirrored her every prayer.

Confidence—inexorable confidence—was the hallmark of my parents.

Mother's preaching was a study in sincerity. In the rising and falling cadences of her hypnotic sermons, there wasn't a shred of doubt or duplicity. She wore her heart on her sleeve. The hungry ate at our table. The homeless slept in our sanctuary.

Father's confidence was reflected in his focus. If the chore at hand was to repair or even build a tractor, he did so with laser-like concentration. Whether it took him a day or a month, he worked until the task was complete. His obsession to understand the underlying mysteries of minerals had him exploring uncharted territory.

Venturing deep into these two territories—the spiritual and the material—defined the excitement of my childhood. As my mother's reputation grew, she accepted invitations to faraway churches and tent revivals. I was thrilled to travel with her. And as my father's molybdenum fixation intensified, I trekked with him to our mine in the middle of nowhere.

Seen through the eyes of a child, these were exotic excursions. Among the first trips I took with Mother was one to Fort Worth, where on the outskirts of the city I watched a tent go up. Workers hammered poles into the earth. A great tarp was anchored and spread. Wooden folding chairs were set in a semicircle. Naked lightbulbs were strung from one side to the other. A makeshift wooden pulpit was placed in the center. A small upright piano was wheeled in. Anticipation was in the air.

I watched the setting sun turn orange, then pink, then violet, then blue-black. People began pouring in—women with children, men who looked lost, the young, the old, the sturdy, the feeble. Black folks came as well.

"Everyone Welcome!" said the sign outside the tent. "Revival meeting tonight! Helen D. Johnson, Evangelist."

I walked to the piano and, with all the force at my command, I struck the opening notes of stirring hymns like "Showers of Blessings," "Oh, How I Love Jesus," and "Just Over in the Glory Land." Because I was a one-girl band, I needed to project. Big chords and big beats were required. I had to get things rolling. Fortunately some folks brought their own tambourines and helped me ride the rhythm. Others began singing along with me. It didn't take long for the Spirit to arrive. Of course it was Mother who encompassed that Spirit and gave it voice.

It was Mother who spoke of the Holy Ghost as a living, breathing force who had swept into the tent, ready to invade our hearts and heads. It was Mother who spoke thrillingly of the glory of God, not a God who punished, but a God who replenished and renewed, a God of hope, a God of salvation, a God whose incomprehensible parental sacrifice proved his love for all his children, a God who could and would and will give our lives new purpose, new meaning, new energy, new joy—a God who, above all, healed both the spirit and the body. Through her love of God, my mother healed with her hands. People came to her in faith—the young, the elderly, the crippled, the blind.

My favorite part of the service, aside from Mother's stirring message, was the altar call. Here I was called upon to sing "Just as I Am." I felt that, in my own small way, I might be able to touch the hearts of those who were hesitant. I saw that the sweeter I sang, the more immediate the response: worshippers rising from their chairs and walking toward Mother to accept the salvation of their Savior.

When the service was over, I felt a great burden had been lifted from the shoulders of people who had entered as strangers but now stood beside my mother as sisters and brothers in Christ. As they exited, I could feel their gratitude. Sometimes, just because my spirit was overflowing, I'd pick up my accordion and play "The Love of God" until the tent was empty and it was just Mother and me standing there. I'd put down my instrument and she'd open her arms. She'd embrace me and say, "Thank you, Mirriam. God has been served."

These were heady days of the great revivalists of the fifties. Traveling the road, from California to Arkansas, from Texas to Tennessee, we would encounter legendary preachers like William Branham. The beloved Brother Branham was a leading light in the post–World War II evangelical movement. There was also Kathryn Kuhlman, another renowned faith healer; and, of course, the incandescent Billy Graham, who removed the ropes segregating whites from blacks at his meetings and, more than anyone in this sacred movement, found universal favor.

When the road wasn't leading to out-of-state revival meetings, it was leading to our twelve-hundred-acre mining property. Those two-hour car trips to the mine were part of the Johnson family lore. We'd load up in Daddy's old Lincoln and head out of Mesa, past Ray (that housed a huge copper mine), past Superior and Kearney, up to the gates of Diamond Ranch, beyond which were the makeshift roads that meandered through the expansive washes. The desert landscape was a wonder to behold, the sun blazing down on rugged rock formations and the graceful Palo Verde and Chilean pine trees as we drove under the imposing silhouette of Superstition Mountain.

The cabin itself, built by Daddy's hands, was a two-story stucco construction near the Gila River. It was basic but comfortable. Daddy and my brothers had also managed to dig a mine shaft. Sometimes they would set off dynamite. The explosive booms could be heard for miles around. We'd take walks around the abandoned railroad tracks and hear stories of Silver Mining Jake and tales of buried gold. Rather than reading a children's story, I felt myself living inside one.

There was also a sense of danger. Climbing the steep mountains, I'd sometimes fall and suffer bloody scrapes. But that didn't stop me or any other family member from exploring. I was once bit by a small but deadly scorpion. Mother immediately prayed for me while Daddy stuck a pin in my finger to extract the bloody venom. I was a little shaken, but fine. According to my sister Sharon, I also swallowed a baby hummingbird. If that is true—and I doubt it—it happened when I was too young to remember. Sharon swore the hummingbird was the source of my musical talent.

Between these twin paths—the path to salvation and the path to discovery—I witnessed two extraordinary beings fully committed to their lifelong truths. My mother and father never tired. Their enthusiasm never lagged. And as they aged, their commitment to their causes only strengthened. Facing the future, they were fearless.

"God will provide," said Mother, in spite of the fact that her congregation was poor and the income derived from her revival meetings was meager.

"I will provide," said Daddy, who, because his mine never resulted in much money, worked a dizzying array of other jobs and other trades.

In the end, God did provide, and so did Daddy.

"Carnal Arnold," Mother would sometimes call him, referring to the fact that he would discuss money matters at the dinner table while she wanted talk to center on our Creator. And yet this divide between husband and wife wasn't really a divide at all. It was more like a bridge built of mutual respect. Mother respected Daddy's mind. Daddy respected Mother's faith. This was the bridge over which I walked as a child, the bridge that led to the world beyond our home, our church, and our mine—the world of Mesa, Arizona, the small city where, in midcentury America, I came of age.

Chapter 3

BEYOND THE MOUNTAINS OF THE MOON

ALTHOUGH FOR MUCH OF MY PROFESSIONAL ADULT LIFE I'D BE associated with rock and roll and outlaw country, I must confess that my cultural influences were not rooted in rebellion. To a large degree, I was a typical fifties girl. I loved Patti Page asking, "How much is that doggie in the window?" I loved Doris Day singing "Que Sera, Sera." I loved Teresa Brewer's "Ricochet Romance," Johnny Mathis's "Chances Are," and Rosemary Clooney's "Hey There." I loved James Dean and June Allyson, Grace Kelly and Gregory Peck. And, of course, like the rest of the universe, I absolutely adored Elvis the minute I saw him on *The Ed Sullivan Show.*

As a budding musician, though, I found that other kinds of music excited my imagination. I remember listening late at night to faraway stations broadcasting black blues that mysteriously accessed my soul. At a young age I learned "St. Louis Blues."

Cowboy culture is an essential part of Arizona. As a girl, I felt that influence. I dressed up like Dale Evans. I considered Roy Rogers heroic. Who could resist a handsome singing cowboy? Yet I wasn't a country music fan. When I heard the classic country crooners like Hank Williams, I was too young to appreciate their profound gifts.

I considered their music corny. My tastes ran to the more modern sounds of Fats Domino's "Blueberry Hill" and Johnnie Ray's "The Little White Cloud That Cried."

Mesa was predominantly Mormon. You'd think that because we were pentecostal Christians I'd be made to feel like an outsider. My mother's mission was totally outside the bounds of the Church of Jesus Christ of Latter-day Saints. Yet I cannot recall a single instance when my faith was called into question by any of my teachers or friends. I proudly and openly believed what I believed. I never tried to hide my identity as an evangelical. All you had to do was come to my home and see the bright white neon sign marking my mother's Lighthouse Mission. Sister Helen was known throughout the region. Yet no one scorned, belittled, or mocked me. My parents assumed that the foundation of my faith was strong enough to withstand the influence of the majority culture. And it was. At least for as long as I lived at home.

Grounded in the love ethos of the living God, Mother had no fear that the secular world would taint my faith. She never restricted my school activities. I could read whatever books and see whatever movies caught my fancy. When I started singing the popular songs of the day, Mother didn't object. At an early age—ten or eleven—I also began writing songs. Some had a religious theme while others didn't. Mother was simply happy that I had found a creative outlet. When it comes to the wider world, pentecostals are not known for being open-minded. But the pentecostal who shaped my world, Helen D. Johnson, was entirely open when her daughter began composing little ditties about teenage heartaches.

Mother also was not hesitant to take me to talent contests at the Big Apple, a ranch-styled restaurant that was a popular spot in the midfifties. There were yodelers, guitarists, jugglers, flamenco dancers, and little ol' me singing "St. Louis Blues." The flamenco dancers won.

The flamenco dancers also won all the talent contests at my junior and high schools where I continued to perform in public. I floated in and out of girl groups appearing on *The Lew King Show*, Mesa's answer to *Ted Mack's Amateur Hour*. I also sang with a variety of bands. In all instances, I was hardly a sensation. At the same time, I felt comfortable onstage and felt little fear—even standing in front of a television camera.

I don't think I had an overabundance of charisma. And I was hardly cocky. I saw my talent realistically: I could play the piano pleasingly; I could write an original song; I could sing on key in a voice that had personality. My own personality was perky, and it came out in my music. I was a happy teenager, delighted to present myself as a budding musical artist. But I had no delusions of grandeur or fantasies of stardom. Of course I wanted to win the contests I entered, but when I didn't, I was fine.

My parents and siblings were especially supportive. They kept insisting I was special. My big brother Paul was always trumpeting my musical achievements. When Mom and Dad weren't available, Paul drove me to the various venues, insisting all the while I was a surefire winner. Sister Sharon felt much the same. Two years my senior, she was a firecracker, a gorgeous young woman who at age sixteen became pregnant by a sailor handsome enough to be a movie star. Becoming a young mother, though, didn't slow Sharon down. She was a rebel and a ringleader. Men adored her. At any given time, at least a half dozen men were hot on her trail.

Sharon had more than style and sex appeal. She knew no strangers. To one intimate degree or another, everyone became her friend. Of course her freewheeling ways put her at odds with Mother, who expected her children to behave with decorum. Even staring at the definition in a dictionary, Sharon didn't know the meaning of *decorum*. She was my parents' wild child.

Without trying, I became the golden child, the gifted one who, as Sister Helen had prophesied, had some special purpose. It wasn't a role I relished, but neither was it a role I rejected. It was hardly a chore to

23

sing in church or join Mother at her revival meetings. It was a privilege that I thoroughly enjoyed. And while I admired Sharon's spunk and welcomed her support, the fact of her pregnancy did much to alert my fourteen-year-old mind to the dangers of promiscuity.

Not that I was shy around boys. By high school, my steady boyfriend was Don Swartz, one of the most popular guys on the football team. Don was tall and lanky, with dreamy brown eyes and a laid-back demeanor. He wasn't a braggart like some of the athletes, and he wasn't too forward. Although we never discussed theology, he took his Mormonism as seriously as I took my religion. He talked about becoming a missionary.

At the same time, my romantic connection to Don was deep enough to describe as love. Not long into our courtship, we professed our love to each other. He was the man I fully expected to marry.

In some ways, we were model teenagers—he a gridiron hero, me a member of the Rabbettes cheering squad. On dates I'd wear cute squaw boots, low-cut Riders, and tight western shirts. In the front seat of his mother's Buick, we'd cuddle up below the big screen at the Pioneer Drive-In, watching in wonder as Charlton Heston commanded his chariot in *Ben Hur* and Rock Hudson pursued Doris Day in *Pillow Talk*. Under a full moon on lover's lane, we made out to the Platters' "Smoke Gets in Your Eyes" and Dion and the Belmonts' "A Teenager in Love." Yet in spite of our intense desire, neither of us dared go all the way.

Were my memory sharper, I could explain exactly how my faith was challenged during my teen years. I'm afraid, though, all I can recall is an indefinite and uncomfortable period of time in which I found myself angry with God. This is hardly unusual for a young person brought up on strict beliefs. But it wasn't the tenets of my mother's religion that I was railing against. It was some amorphous complaint that had me uneasy. And like all mortal souls, I harbored some doubts.

The perpetual presence of evil was a concept with which I struggled. If God were all-powerful, wouldn't he use that power to destroy evil? Of course Mother had answers for such questions—that goodness could only be seen in contrast to evil; that without darkness we could never understand the beauty of light; that the actual power of evil was a deception, not a reality; that love inevitably trumps hate; and that, finally, the ways of God are embedded in sacred mystery. Our job is only to seek knowledge of his will.

Her answers mostly—but not always—satisfied my curious mind. Even as a youngster I was a serious thinker. I loved books that provoked questions—Frances Hodgson Burnett's *The Secret Garden* and coming-of-age novels like Charlotte Brontë's *Jane Eyre*, which moved me to consider the forces that form our moral character. I adored the rhythms and rhymes of poetry, especially Edgar Allan Poe's. With great wonder and delight I read and reread his evocative "Eldorado"—a story that I envisioned unfolding in the wilderness of Arizona. In "Eldorado" a gallant knight searches for the fabled lost city of gold, only to receive mystical directions from a ghost, a "pilgrim shadow":

> *"Over the Mountains*
> *Of the Moon,*
> *Down the Valley of the Shadow,*
> *Ride, boldly ride,"*
> *The shade replied,*
> *"If you seek for Eldorado!"*[1]

It's no surprise that the poem would appeal to the daughter of a miner and a minister. It's all about the insoluble mystery of seeking—seeking precious minerals, seeking the majesty of God, seeking that which, although invisible, will finally satisfy our lifelong quest.

Even as a young person, I found my thoughts centering on weighty matters. I wondered, for example, about the nature of eternity. What did infinity mean? What did infinity look like? I was fascinated by time. Could time ever be stopped, ever be caught like a fluttering butterfly and held in a jar? What would it mean to hold time in my hand? And how could time ever be expanded? Could a minute ever last longer than a minute? Could a second last longer than a second?

I was conscious of the passing of time. The years between ages fifteen and sixteen, sixteen and seventeen, went by in a flash. I was in love with Don but then Don was gone. Love hadn't lasted. More reliable was my love of music. That love led me to do something I didn't think I'd ever dare. With friends I snuck off and went to a rough club in Phoenix called the Riverside. Johnny Cash was performing. I didn't drink and I don't think I even danced. But I knew this wasn't the kind of scene that would meet Mother's approval.

Something bigger than Mother's approval, though, got me going. I wanted to hear, see, and feel the presence of a singer like Johnny Cash. In those early days, he was associated with Elvis, Jerry Lee Lewis, and Carl Perkins. These were cutting-edge artists. They were changing music in ways that stimulated my imagination. Seeing Johnny raise the roof at the Riverside was something I'd never forget.

I was fascinated by how he cradled the guitar while moving it side to side, as though he was rocking a baby in his arms. His voice sounded rough and smooth, all at the same time. I could feel his sincerity. Watching him command the stage, I saw a driven man who at this point in his career was just coming around the bend and finding great fame.

These were the days—the late fifties—when rock and roll was still a burgeoning phenomenon. I didn't think in categories then—and still don't—but I did see all that music as my music, music I loved and music I could both write and sing. By "rock and roll" I mean more than just Bill Haley or Bo Diddley. By rock and roll I simply mean music embraced by teenagers, everything from Buddy Holly's "Rave On!" to the Everly Brothers' "Dream On" to Elvis's "Love Me Tender"—and even to salty country-sounding songs like Patsy Cline's "Walkin' After Midnight."

I felt the pull of this music, its powerful rhythms and urgent stories. The fact that I would soon be swept up into its swirling orbit was one of the great surprises of my early life. The way that came about speaks to the enigma of fate. Circumstances conspired to put me in a special place at a special time. Looking back, I'm amazed by those circumstances. But more than the circumstances, I'm amazed by my own daring to follow a path shrouded in mystery. Without realizing it, like the knight in Poe's "Eldorado," I was searching for something just beyond the mountains of the moon.

Chapter 4

YOUNG AND INNOCENT

WHILE I DISPLAYED A HEALTHY DEGREE OF DETERMINATION and confidence, I was far from obsessed with forging a musical career at age eighteen. In fact, I looked on it as mere fun. It was a wonderful diversion to be able to write and sing songs.

Because I had sung in church for so long—and with such enthusiastic support from everyone around me—I viewed audiences lovingly. I presumed that, like my fellow worshippers, they were on my side. Meanwhile, my brother Paul and sister Sharon presumed that I was more talented than I judged myself to be. Where I was a little casual when it came to presenting myself in public, they were assertive. They felt that the world needed to know about me, and given any opportunity they brashly sang my praise.

Sharon was especially vocal. She had precociously entered the world of barrooms and nightclubs where, in her effusive way, she befriended a large number of men. Many of these friendships led to high drama. Sharon specialized in high drama. But because she was essentially a good-hearted soul who loved connecting people she liked, she saw that one of these friendships could benefit me.

Easy Deal Wilson, a man Sharon would later marry, was a piano-playing, saloon-owning character. Like Sharon, Easy Deal was an ongoing lover of life whose circle of contacts in the Valley of the Sun—the greater Phoenix metropolitan area—was extensive. In our corner of the world, he knew everyone there was to know in the entertainment business.

"Easy Deal knows Duane Eddy," said Sharon, "and Duane's looking for a singer to produce."

A major pop star in the late fifties, Eddy had pioneered a distinctive low-note guitar sound—a twangy effect—that had a major impact on rock and roll. One note and you knew it was Duane Eddy. With the help of producer Lee Hazlewood, he had turned out a long string of hits—"Rebel Rouser," "Ramrod," "Cannonball," "Peter Gunn," "Forty Miles of Bad Road," "Because They're Young," and "Shazam!"—flavored with a guitar tone all its own.

At the time, I had only a passing familiarity with these hits. I didn't really understand Duane's importance in the music universe. His name, however, did make an impression. Sharon knew more about him than I did. She said that although he was always out on tour, he kept a place in Phoenix where he had moved with his parents as a teenager. In 1960, the year we met, Duane was twenty-two and I was seventeen.

Sharon made the arrangements: Easy Deal would bring Duane to his place to audition me. My protective brother Paul, who liked to call himself my manager—even if there wasn't much to manage—would not allow me to go unescorted. It was a sunny afternoon when Paul and I entered the dark barroom.

Bubbly as ever, Sharon was there and introduced me to Easy Deal. The first thing I noticed was that he was missing a few essential teeth. His skin was wrinkled and his eyes watery.

"Sharon brags on you all the time," he was quick to say. "You best be as good as she says you are."

"She's even better," Paul insisted.

"She's the best," Sharon chimed in. "Where's Duane Eddy?"

"On his way," Easy Deal assured her.

"Sharon says you have a piano," I said.

"Naturally. What kind of saloon would I be running without a piano? Got me a good one right over there."

In the back of the club was an old rinky-dink upright. The ivory was chipped on many of the keys. When I hit the first chord, the sound startled me. The instrument was wildly out of tune.

Sensing my discontent, Easy Deal assured me, "The crowd that comes in here just likes their music loud. Long as they can hear it, they like it."

I smiled politely and said it would do. What choice did I have?

I was warming up when Duane arrived. He was a good-looking man with slicked-up hair in the wavy style of teen idols like Fabian, Bobby Rydell, and Ricky Nelson. He was neatly dressed in a dark shirt and dark trousers. His smile was warm and his demeanor shy. He politely thanked me for coming to the club and thanked my brother for accompanying me. Although he was still a young man, he had the aura of a family man. Later I learned that he was. He was married with two children. There was something straight-ahead and serious about Duane.

Duane, Paul, Sharon, and Easy Deal sat at a table facing the piano.

"Let's see what this little girl can do," said Easy Deal.

"Take your time," said Duane. "Whenever you're ready."

I'd been playing "St. Louis Blues" for years. It was a song I knew inside out. Why not go with a sure thing? So I sang it, accompanying myself with big strong chords while giving the tune a rocking rhythm.

When I was through, Sharon and Paul jumped up and gave me a rousing hand. No big surprise there. They were my biggest boosters. But what did Duane think?

"That poor piano could use a tuning," he said, "but you made it work anyway. Great rendition. Great playing. Great singing. I'm just wondering if you have any songs of your own?"

Delighted with his reaction, my answer was, "Yes."

"You mind playing a few?"

"I'd love to."

I played a set of original songs with my usual confidence. I thought they were fine but had no great expectations that Duane would like them. They were love songs and a far cry from "Rebel Rouser" and "Peter Gunn." Yet Duane did like them.

"I like them a lot," he was quick to say. "I think you have talent, Mirriam Johnson, and I'd like to work with you."

I wasn't sure what that meant. I was still a junior in high school. I guess Duane must have seen the confusion on my face.

"I want you to finish school for sure," he said. "That's important. But over the coming months I'd like to help you. There's no rush. We'll take our time. The last thing I want to do is disturb your life. But I would like you to know—and I'd like to let your folks know as well—that I see you as someone with big potential. And I see myself as someone who can help you fulfill that potential."

"Well, this is perfect!" Sharon shouted. "This is wonderful! This is the start of something great!"

Of course validation always feels good, and coming from an established star—the first such star, by the way, that I had ever met—I couldn't help but be excited.

The excitement was sustained when Duane proved true to his word. Before leaving on tour, he made a point to visit our home where he explained to my parents his interest in my artistic potential. Mother and Daddy were impressed that a well-mannered gentleman spoke respectfully and admiringly of their daughter. They liked Duane. On occasion, he came to Mother's church. Other times, Duane took me into the studio where we began recording my songs.

"I don't want to give you too much direction," he said, "because

I really believe you're a natural. You write and sing from the heart. That's something that can't be taught or learned. You either have it or you don't. You have it, Mirriam. It's just a matter of placing you in the right musical setting."

We went into Audio Recorders, a legendary studio where great producers like Phil Spector had worked. Duane backed me up along with great saxophonists King Curtis and Jim Horn, both of whom would go on to play with Aretha. The level of musicianship was extraordinary. I sang "Lonesome Road" by Gene Austin and a tune written by Larry Knechtel—who later played in the band Bread—that summed up my life at that very moment: "Young and Innocent."

Chapter 5

THE END OF INNOCENCE

DEATH MARKS THE END OF INNOCENCE. TO THE YOUNG, DEATH
is a remote concept unconnected to our reality. But when death comes
to your home, that reality is shaken and the world feels very different.

On August 15, 1960, a deputy sheriff knocked on our door.

"Are you the parents of Paul Johnson?"

"Yes," said my father.

"It pains me to say that your son was killed instantly when his
Austin-Healey hit a telegraph pole near 68th and Camelback."

Daddy was stoic. We all stood silent. We couldn't believe the words
we heard. The loss was too great to comprehend.

The truth was that David was known as the drinker among my
siblings. Several times my folks had to bail him out of trouble. And
while I knew that Paul, the son of a race-car driver, liked to speed on
the open road, I couldn't recall a time when he had been inebriated
in my company. In fact, his sober consistency and singular support
of my music were some of my great comforts. Now, without warning,
that comfort was gone. For all of us who loved and cherished his
sweet and generous soul, the mourning would last a lifetime. Paul

died two months before his twenty-fourth birthday. The grieving was done in private—Daddy retreating to his mining property, Mama holding forth at her revival meetings, bringing lost souls to Christ and amazingly withstanding the loss of her beloved son. After the funeral, I went alone to his grave and stood there the better part of the afternoon, crying my heart out.

His passing came in the wake of meeting Duane. Paul not only chaperoned that encounter, he encouraged me to continue working with Duane.

"The man understands you," he had told me after that initial audition at Easy Deal's. "The man appreciates you. I think he's someone you can trust."

Paul's approval of Duane held great weight with me. With Paul gone, I was suddenly missing the man guiding my nascent musical career. It's no wonder I began to lean on Duane for that support. And for his part, Duane was more than willing to lend that support; he was demonstrably eager.

Ten months after Paul's death, in the summer of 1961, I graduated from high school. It was around this same time that my single of "Lonesome Road" and "Young and Innocent" was released on Jamie Records. This was heady stuff for eighteen-year-old Mirriam Johnson. It was one thing to have sung in church, at revival meetings, and at local talent shows. It was quite another to be holding a 45-rpm, seven-inch disc carrying my name.

What's more, Duane expressed interest in helping me sell songs that I had composed.

"I think you can have a two-prong career," he said. "One as a singer, and another as a writer. I'd be surprised if you didn't succeed in both fields."

He carefully listened as I played him my songs on the piano. He had very few suggestions—a minor edit here or there.

"Chet Atkins is a good friend," he said. "I think Chet would like these songs. Chet may be able to place them."

Chet Atkins, of course, was not only one of the premier guitarists in the country, but a powerhouse Nashville producer.

Things were moving fast—so fast, in fact, that I wondered whether Mother or Daddy might call a halt to it all, especially when, after Duane divorced his wife, he made it clear that his interest in me went beyond my music.

It is a testimony to my parents' wisdom that they were not alarmed by the prospect of their young and innocent daughter venturing into the mysterious world of show business. Perhaps it was because they trusted me, or perhaps because, as adventurous souls themselves, they were incapable of denying me such a great adventure.

In Mother's case, it is extraordinary that she did nothing—either by word or by deed—to stop me. Given her overwhelming passion for her ministry—and the fact that for so long I was an integral part of that ministry—you might imagine her balking. You might imagine her insisting that I not leave her side to pursue secular music. You might think that she would rant about the sins of the material world and do all she could to keep me out of that world.

But Mother's wisdom was deep. She understood that mothers, unlike God, have limitations. She recognized the complexity of life choices. She knew that children choose different paths. And most powerfully, she understood the difference between ego and faith. Ego would mean imposing *her* will. Faith would mean following *God's* will. And God's will, especially as applied to others, is not always crystal clear. God's will requires thoughtful prayer. And no one was more committed to thoughtful prayer than my mother.

What were my prayers at this critical time in my life? What was in my secret heart?

I know I didn't pray for fortune and fame. Fortune and fame have never been fantasies of mine, no matter my age. I prayed only that my life continue to take an adventurous turn. I prayed that the spirit imbued in my parents—the spirit that had them venturing forth into the wide-open spaces of the glorious deserts and mountains of Arizona—be imbued in me. I prayed that my life not be boring or predictable.

In that sense, I'm glad to report that all my prayers came true.

Chapter 6

MEET MIRRIAM EDDY

DURING OUR COURTSHIP, DUANE WAS THE VERY MODEL OF decorum. Never overly aggressive. No sudden moves. Relaxed, self-assured, and considerate. I had no reason for alarm.

Why, then, was I alarmed when, on one of our first dates, we drove straight out into the Arizona wilderness for miles on end? Not only had I been in no-man's-land before, but my father's mine was situated in such a spot. Much of my childhood had been spent gazing at the star-filled sky far from the lights of the city. So why worry now? Why insist, after driving more than an hour, that he turn around and take me home immediately?

For one thing, I was alone in a car with an older man with strong feelings for me. How well did I really know him? How far could I trust him? How could I know that he wasn't going to pull over on some remote wash and take advantage of me?

As it turned out, these were the unfounded fears of a teenage girl who had lived a sheltered life under the strong protection of loving parents. All Duane wanted to do was treat me to dinner at a mesquite grill over on Pinnacle Peak. In fact, the Pinnacle Peak Patio did turn out the tastiest cowboy steaks in the state.

We arrived just as the last sliver of sun was visible on the vast western landscape. The sky turned from purple to dark, brooding blue. When darkness finally fell, the enormous sky—aglow with a half moon and a million glittering stars—surrounded us.

"It's a big, wide world out there," said Duane, finishing off his steak.

"I like the quiet," I said. "I like the view from here. I like everything about Arizona."

"I was talking about the world outside Arizona. Like New York. Like California. Like London. You'd like all those places, Mirriam."

"I'm sure I would."

"And I'd like to show them to you. What do you say?"

What could I say? I was flattered. I was excited. I was young.

"Would you consider joining my show and going on the road?" he asked.

"Of course I would," I said. "But are you sure I'd fit in with your band?"

"I'd feature you," he promised. "I believe my fans would get a kick out of you. In fact, I know they would."

This was the summer of 1961, weeks after I'd graduated from high school. My Don Swartz romance was over. Duane's marriage was over. It felt like a good time for a new beginning.

"Naturally I'd have to ask my parents," I said.

"I wouldn't do it without their permission," Duane affirmed.

On the long road back over the desert, in the dark of night, we didn't say much to each other. We didn't have to. At that point we were seeing my future in the same way. My future was music.

It was the beginning of the New Frontier. Jack Kennedy was the newly elected, youngest president ever. Youth was a prized commodity. Hope was in the air. Rock and roll was on the radio.

In the fall of 1961 and the winter of 1962, I traveled with Duane

Eddy, who during that tour declared his love for me and became my boyfriend. I was excited by both this new romance and our travels around the country. We performed in places that seemed glamorous to a girl from small-town Arizona—Chicago, Atlantic City, New York City, Philadelphia.

In Philly, for example, I appeared on *American Bandstand* where Dick Clark, a close friend of Duane's, greeted me with great enthusiasm. He plugged my records shamelessly and proved to be one of my most loyal supporters.

We played on shows with the top pop artists of the day—Chubby Checker and the Shirelles who were super-hot with "Will You Love Me Tomorrow?" and "Dedicated to the One I Love." When we shared the stage with Brenda Lee, I could see that she, like many of the girls, had a crush on Duane. In New York we stayed at the swank Warwick Hotel where in a few years the Beatles, friends of Duane's, held some of their famous press conferences.

Duane, of course, was the star—and much admired by his colleagues like the Beach Boys, Bobby Darin, and even Elvis. Duane was respected as an early architect of rock. I was content to be a featured part of his show and sing my singles like "Lonesome Road" and "Young and Innocent." When those singles didn't take off, I was fine. And so was Duane.

"It takes a while to build a career," he told me. "And you've taken all the right first steps."

Career-building, though, was not one of my concerns. I was simply content to get a firsthand view of this new world of high-powered show business. I liked the always-on-the-go fast-moving energy. I liked flying off to exotic new places and meeting exotic new people—artists, agents, promoters. The cast of characters was colorful. I saw that my prayer—for an adventurous life—had been answered. And I was grateful.

I was especially grateful for Duane's attention. He was a fine mentor. He knew music in a way that I did not. I was fascinated to learn that, although famous for rock music, Duane had great esteem for country music, a genre I had largely ignored. He pointed me in the direction of country artists like Don Gibson, a singer-songwriter famous for "Sweet Dreams" and "I Can't Stop Loving You." I became enamored of Gibson's vocal phrasing. To hear him sing "Just One More Time" or "Sea of Heartbreak" or "Lonesome Me" was a revelation. He had this wonderfully relaxed rhythm, a silky-smooth voice, and a beautifully laid-back sense of storytelling. I carefully studied his approach and, of all the singers of the late fifties and early sixties, I'd say Gibson influenced me most deeply.

Duane made me realize that I had a lot to learn when it came to country. I knew little about its history or even the work of current artists like George Jones, another singer I came to adore. It didn't take me long to realize that George was a giant of American music, one of the most profound writers and brilliant singers ever to grace a stage. Later in life I'd get to know George well, but in these early years he was a far-off guiding light and powerful inspiration.

When we traveled to Nashville, Duane made good on his promise to introduce me to his pal Chet Atkins, an altogether decent man. Chet was from the mountains of Tennessee and never lost that country-boy charm. He was tall and slender, with high cheekbones, blue eyes, and light brown hair. His tempo and temper were always extremely laid-back. When he got lost in thought, his eyes would start blinking at double-speed.

After I sang him a few of my compositions, he said, "Your songs are good. You have talent. Keep writing and keep sending me your stuff. I think I can place them with country artists and maybe pop artists too. Don't worry about category. Just write what you feel."

"That's all I know how to do," I confessed.

At the same time, Chet did not sign me up as a solo artist. He had that power. As head producer at RCA, he could sign whomever he pleased. I don't know if that disappointed Duane. I know it did not disappoint me. My expectations remained low to nonexistent. An encouraging word about my songwriting from a leading industry light was all I needed.

It was during that initial tour that Duane proposed. I wasn't surprised but, at the same time, I wasn't without doubts. On the plus side, Duane was a great guy. He was smart, he was talented, he was handsome, and he was certainly supportive of me. But love? I looked back at love as something I had for my high school heartthrob Don Swartz. Love meant head-over-heels love, dream-of-you-night-and-day love, can't-live-without-you love. True, my love for Don was an immature love, a love that didn't last, but I kept referring to it because it was the only romantic love I had ever known.

Did I love Duane? Well, I had great fondness for him. I was grateful to him. I enjoyed his company. I liked him enormously, but *love*—the real deal, heart-stopping, dream-making love? No, I didn't feel that kind of love for him. But then some thoughts came to mind: *Maybe marrying love and romantic love are two different things. Maybe romantic love belongs to high school. Maybe that's not the love that binds a marriage. Maybe marrying love rightly describes my feelings for Duane. Maybe marrying love is mature love. You don't have to be giddy. You don't have to be weak in the knees. No stars in your eyes. No romantic intoxication. Simply like and respect a man a great deal, a man whom you are certain likes and respects you—and, most importantly, a man who says he loves you.*

Duane's feelings for me were certainly more blatant—more effusive and romantic—than mine for him. But rather than view that as a problem, I saw it as a plus. Someone had once spoken words that registered in my psyche: *Always marry someone who loves you more than you love him.* Remembering those words made my decision easier.

"Yes," I told Duane, "I will marry you."

"Vegas is a marrying town," said Duane. "Any objections to Vegas?"

"None."

Vegas provided a certain glamour. Vegas was glitzy, Vegas was fun, Vegas was an upcoming hot spot of American entertainment—and close to Arizona. Duane booked a palatial suite at the Tropicana Hotel. My family was there. Among the few other guests was Dick Clark, who served as Duane's best man.

I cannot recall any discussions about marrying in a church. My parents offered no objections. They understood, as did I, that, given the show-business culture I had entered, Vegas was the place.

Although Duane's parents lived there, Phoenix was not a place where we wanted to settle. He had his hopes set on Los Angeles. After long years of grueling tours, he wanted to concentrate on building his publishing business. The idea was to develop a deep catalog of songs that would provide long-term income. He was also interested in taking new artists into the studio as a producer.

As a singer-songwriter, I fit into Duane's plans quite nicely. And as far as LA went, I was game. I'd miss my family, but Southern California was an hour's plane ride away. Besides, the notion of living in Los Angeles was intriguing. The City of Angels was uncharted territory. I knew little about it. Duane knew a host of fascinating people there. He spoke of them fondly and assured me I'd like them. No doubt I would.

Once I arrived, though, I found myself harboring other doubts—new doubts, nagging doubts, unexpected doubts that turned my spiritual life upside down and inside out.

Chapter 7

THE CANYONS

OUR FIRST HOME, A RENTAL, WAS IN LAUREL CANYON, THE lovely rustic area just north of West Hollywood that cuts through the hills leading to the San Fernando Valley. This was the first permanent place I had lived outside my childhood home in Mesa. The contrast could not have been greater.

The stark rough-and-tumble topography of Arizona was all about uncultivated beauty, the rugged sculpture of centuries-old rock and stone, the mysteries of copper mines hidden beneath jagged mountains. The landscape of Los Angeles was all about cultivated beauty, the importation of palm trees and exotic plants to re-dress what had once been a desert. As a child, I learned to love nature in the raw. As a young married woman, I learned to appreciate nature as modified by man. I say "appreciate," not "love," because, in truth, I never learned to love Los Angeles.

Nor, I must admit, did I ever learn to love my husband in a way that I could call complete. Still hanging over my head was that sense of love as something both wildly romantic and emotionally obsessive. Since Duane was my first and only lover, I also had no way of comparing our sexual rapport to anything else. Sex seemed little more than perfunctory. There were no fireworks, and no way to know whether it was because of him or me. Maybe the chemistry simply wasn't there. Or maybe my inexperienced mind rationalized that marital sex, like marital love, didn't have to be explosive or all-consuming.

I had no reason to complain about the lush lifestyle to which Duane had introduced me. Our comfortable and charming Laurel Canyon home was designed in the style of a Swiss chalet. It was exciting to learn that Henry Mancini, one of America's leading composers, was a nearby neighbor.

Even more exciting was the fact that my own compositions, encouraged by Duane, were getting out there in the world. I found it easy to work on the Baldwin Acrosonic spinet in our living room. In those early years in Los Angeles, it was especially satisfying when Chet Atkins proved true to his word and took several of my songs. This came at a time when, thanks to Duane, I had gone to my first George Jones show. As a result of listening to George, I was writing with a decidedly country flavor. Chet got Dottie West, then a rising country star, to record my "No Sign of the Living" and Hank Locklin, the Grand Ole Opry stalwart, to cut "I'm Blue."

"But you aren't just country," said Chet. "I think you can write pop songs as well."

I saw Chet was right when Nancy Sinatra sang my "If He'd Love Me" for her father's Reprise Records. It wasn't a big hit like "These Boots Are Made for Walkin'," but the writer and producer of "Boots," Lee Hazelwood, sang his own version of my "I'm Blue" as a solo artist, also for Reprise.

"You'll have lots of hits," said Chet. "Just keep writing."

Writing and reading became my refuge, especially when I became pregnant a few months after my twentieth birthday in the summer of 1963. Writing brought me enormous joy, and reading brought me into an intellectual realm I had never before known.

Duane himself was a serious reader and deep thinker. He surrounded himself with smart show-business friends like the wonderful singing duo Don and Phil Everly. Of the two brothers, Phil was the talkative one, an engaging character who often bemoaned the ongoing conflicts between him and Don. Lou Adler, then managing the Mamas and the Papas, was also part of our social circle, which included a number of psychologists and academics. In his own low-key way, Duane had a point of view he was interested in promulgating.

That point of view was best expressed by two key figures—the author Ayn Rand and the psychotherapist Nathaniel Branden, Rand's former lover and founder of an institute promoting Rand's philosophy known as objectivism. Rand had found fame by writing two bestselling novels: *The Fountainhead*, published in 1943 and turned into a film with Gary Cooper in 1949; and *Atlas Shrugged*, published in 1957. At Duane's suggestion, I read them both. I was intrigued.

"What's most intriguing," said Duane, "is the thinking behind the story—Rand's view of human behavior."

The friends who often congregated at our home were, like Duane, devotees of Rand. Several were psychologists who had worked under Branden's tutelage. They were filled with enthusiasm for objectivism. They were the first genuine intellectuals I had ever known and entered my life at a time when I was especially impressionable.

Rand's books were more than entertaining reads. They were replete with provocative ideas. For example, the lead character in *The Fountainhead*, Frank Roark, is an architect modeled on Frank Lloyd Wright. Modern architecture is a central theme. Modern man is even more of a central theme. Rand saw the ideal modern man as someone reliant on no one but himself. He is a prime mover whose integrity derives from not only his own values but his self-interest.

One of Rand's most famous tracts is entitled "The Value of Selfishness." The six pillars of self-esteem are conscious living, self-acceptance, self-responsibility, self-assertiveness, living purposely, and personal integrity. There is no mention of God, no acknowledgment of a higher power, no allusion to a mystical or spiritual force to undergird our behavior and, of course, no acknowledgment of Jesus Christ.

Given my background, you might think that such a philosophy would repel me. In fact, it attracted me. It may have been the new circumstances surrounding me—new husband, new city, new culture, new friends. Or it may just have been that this was my first in-depth exposure to a system of beliefs not defined by my mother. The truth is that I had never read psychology or philosophy before. The age of a college student—an age when attitudes swiftly shift and struggles with self-identity are rampant—I was an eager reader, willing to consider what seemed a sophisticated and measured means of adjudicating human behavior. As my first taste of exotic intellectualism, objectivism was intoxicating.

I certainly did not share these new thoughts with Mother. When she called from Mesa, our conversations were short. She asked about my health, Duane's health, and whether I was happy. I said I was. I told her about the songs I was writing and mentioned that our social life was amusing. During that summer of 1963, when I told her I was pregnant, she was overjoyed, as was I.

In November of that same year, Duane and I traveled to London, where we learned on the twenty-second that John Kennedy had been assassinated in Dallas. The violent end of the New Frontier came as a shock. Not overtly political, I nonetheless shared the sentiments of most Americans who saw Kennedy as a beacon of hope. Shattered hope followed for years to come. The country was entering a dark period of uncertainty and fear.

Back in Los Angeles, I awaited the birth of my first child with great anticipation. Duane and I had moved to another canyon, this one called Coldwater, that ran north through Beverly Hills, an even more prestigious area than Laurel Canyon. Robert Mitchum lived on the corner. Though I don't remember seeing him, I was excited to know that he was a neighbor. Our new home on Betty Lane was larger and far more modern than our first.

My close friend was the actress Shelley Fabares, at the time married to Lou Adler. A wonderful woman, Shelley was famous for her role as the daughter in *The Donna Reed Show* and had also costarred in three of Elvis's films. It was through her that I met Annette Funicello, Shelley's best friend. The three of us had great times together.

On April 5, 1964, our darling Jennifer was born. Though in these early years I had been excited to travel with Duane through Europe, that excitement couldn't compare to the joy I derived from staying home and tending to my precious infant. Life suddenly had new meaning. Motherhood became my first priority.

When my parents came to visit Beverly Hills, they were pleased with my surroundings but not overly impressed by my lifestyle. They had their own preoccupations—Mother's church, Daddy's mine—and didn't stay long. While they were there, though, they lavished love on their granddaughter. I'm sure Mother saw the large number of secular books around the house. As she was a highly intuitive person, I'm certain she sensed the philosophical shift I was experiencing. Duane had never hidden his own intellectual interests. And yet, not a word from Mother. No warning, no scolding, no recriminations.

"We love you, Mirriam, and always will," was all she said. "We're proud to see you've become a wonderfully caring mother."

Of course both she and Daddy were wonderfully caring grandparents. But, looking back at this period, I'm amazed that Mother was careful not to challenge my forays into non-Christian thinking. She understood what most people wholly committed to a specific theology do not understand: that there are times to approach a nonbeliever and times not to. To understand that requires maximum sensitivity. It requires that you truly put yourself in the other person's place to see whether words, no matter how eloquent, would make a difference.

Mother, who knew me better than anyone, understood that I was going through a transition where I couldn't be reached. And she was right. Her ego was such that she understood the limitations of her power to persuade. For a minister this is a rare recognition.

A nonbeliever. Is that what I had become? To see those words in black and white is unnerving, but they do apply. At the start of my twenties, I entered what would prove to be a long period of agnosticism. Whatever faith I had as a child and teenager fell away before an onslaught of skepticism about the pertinence of the Scriptures to my new life.

New Age thinking in its various forms called to me in books and lectures, many by the apostles of Ayn Rand and Nathaniel Branden.

I do not fault or blame Duane. He never manipulated or cajoled me toward his philosophical leanings. I was a willing follower. I liked all the intellectual intercourse, the long discussions into the nature of logic and reason with people who boasted graduate degrees and spoke with enchanting eloquence. As I write now, I am tempted to call these same people pseudo-intellectuals—and that includes me. But at the time my critical acumen was nonexistent. I was happy to go along for the ride.

There were delightful evenings at home. Many were the times we'd sit together—Duane sipping Scotch, me sipping wine—while listening to the records of the great Spanish guitarist Andrés Segovia playing the fugues of Bach or the preludes of Chopin. Ever the devoted mentor, Duane did more than introduce me to the wonders of classical music. He was also quick to point out popular performers he considered worthy of attention.

One of those performers was Waylon Jennings.

Chapter 8

CRY SOFTLY

My solace was the piano at which, for hours on end, I'd play, sing, and compose. Some of the songs were disposable, but others were good. The good ones were the deep ones, the ones that emanated from the depths of my secret heart.

What secrets did my heart contain?

The biggest secret was my dissatisfaction with a marriage that never grew into anything more than a meaningful friendship. That indefinable element called romance remained elusive. Fondness, yes. Respect, yes. Musical stimulation, intellectual stimulation, social stimulation— yes, yes, yes. But no, I could not say in the silence of my heart that I was in love with my husband. And the inability to make that claim weighed heavily on my days and nights.

It could be morning when Jennifer was napping or evening after I'd prepared dinner and put her to sleep. But at least five or six times during the week I'd go to the keyboard and allow the feelings coursing through me to find expression.

It was satisfying to know that some of my songs had been recorded by Dottie West and Nancy Sinatra, but I wasn't then—and am not now—the kind of writer who consciously composes songs for others to sing. By nature, I'm an autobiographical writer. I write out of my feelings. Even more specifically, I write out of what I'm feeling at the very moment that I'm writing. I write in the *now*. I write in reaction to whatever spirit is passing through me. I try not to scrutinize, judge, or suppress that spirit. My job is simply to give that spirit form.

I wrote the song "Cry Softly" during this period when music was the only means I used to express my sorrow. Otherwise, I was my usual upbeat self. A happy person all my life, I maintained my happy disposition. I wasn't one to cry the blues to family or friends. Instead, those blues were contained in my song that said, "Cry softly, move slowly—away from the man standing there." Because the stories in songs are cryptically rendered, I didn't have to name names. I could convey true feelings without revealing the specifics of my true-life situation.

Even when Duane listened to these songs, many of which were sad, I'm not sure he got it. I'm not sure he heard the genuine discontent that was motivating my music. We didn't discuss our relationship. We didn't seek counsel of any sort. Given the presence of so many psychologists in our circle, you might think that peculiar. Why not seek their help? The answer is that I saw those people as friends. I'd have been embarrassed to sit in their offices and speak of intimate personal problems. Neither Duane nor I was raised to seek psychiatric help.

My husband had to see, however, that I had begun distancing myself from him. Duane, who was dealing with a number of professional frustrations, began to grow jealous. Over time, his jealousy grew to excessive proportions. Duane had nothing to be jealous about. I had no suitors. There were no flirtations. I stayed true to him and my duties as a wife and mother. If you had asked me how I intended to stay in what I saw as a loveless marriage, I could not have answered. Instead, I would have simply gone to the piano to write another sad song.

In 1966, Duane brought home an album by Waylon Jennings, his first on RCA, entitled *Folk-Country*. The cover carried a color photograph of a strikingly handsome man with dark, wavy, slicked-back hair. He wore a white shirt and a sharp gray-and-brown suede jacket. In his arms he held an acoustic guitar.

"RCA is calling him 'folk country' to cash in on the folkie craze," said Duane, "but Waylon really doesn't fit into any category. He's really just a rocker. He rocks between country and rock and roll. But he's also a great ballad singer. I think he's one of the best young artists out there. Give it a listen."

I did, and I immediately agreed with Duane. I loved how Waylon's melodies had a way of weaving in minor chords. I loved how the first single off the record—"That's the Chance I'll Have to Take"—opened with the lines, "Troubles and a worried mind, it seems that's all I've known, but now I'll leave all that behind. . . ." I loved his muscular voice and his insistent rhythms when he sang songs like "What Makes a Man Wander." I could feel his wandering soul. His music was filled with mystery.

I read the album notes that said only six years earlier he had been working as a deejay at a radio station in Lubbock, Texas, before country singer Bobby Bare had introduced him to Chet Atkins, the same Chet Atkins who was listed as producer of this record.

"Waylon's been living in Phoenix," said Duane.

"He has?"

"He's been working at that huge two-story club called JD's."

"I know JD's," I said. "It's between Tempe and Scottsdale, not far from Arizona State."

"Those college kids are crazy for him. He's become a local hero. Next time we go home to visit your folks, we'll go by and tell him hello. You might even want to play him some of your songs."

Although neither Duane nor I would admit it, our marriage was slowly unraveling. But who wants to admit failure, especially failure at something as important as your primary relationship? As the tensions between us intensified, our communication broke down. The lack of passion took its toll. Rather than talk about it, we brooded. And rather than seek to understand the source of the brooding, we remained silent. Resentments built. Anxieties deepened.

I wouldn't have said so then, but the abandonment of my faith was a huge contribution to my unhappiness. Not that I believe a return to Christianity would have salvaged my marriage. Nothing could have saved it. It was a mistake—my mistake—from the start. But the replacement of my faith with a battery of half-beliefs that centered on self as salvation provided little comfort. My mind might have been stimulated, but my soul remained starved for a love that esoteric metaphysical theories couldn't provide. And yet philosophically I continued to stray. I put my Bible aside. I had no interest in attending church. And concerning God, well, God was part of my childhood. Now I was grown.

And now, to take a break from what had become our stagnated life in Los Angeles, we went back to Phoenix for a visit. My mother could tell that I was hurting, but she also detected that I was in no mood to discuss any deficiencies in my life. Rather than probe the reasons behind my discontent, she turned her attention on Jennifer, whom she lavished with love.

A few days after we arrived, Duane mentioned that Waylon Jennings was presently in Phoenix working at Audio Recorders.

"You know that song you just wrote, the one called 'Living Proof'?" said Duane. "You might want to demo it while we're here. You and Waylon could sing it as a duet."

I liked the idea. I loved Waylon's singing style and thought that our voices might blend well together.

When we walked into the studio, Waylon greeted us warmly. He was a big, gregarious guy with an easy grin and a ready wit. I felt as if I'd known him for years. This was the ruggedly good-looking, clean-shaven Waylon, his wavy hair slicked back and his eyes full of fire. Though he had a booming, larger-than-life personality, he showed Duane great respect. You could sense the high regard these men had for each other.

Waylon was in the middle of recording a cover of the Beatles's "Norwegian Wood."

"Interesting song for a country artist," I whispered to Duane.

"I told you that he's more than country," said Duane. "You can't put this guy in a box. His music is all over the place."

Yet his music was incredibly concentrated. His version of "Norwegian Wood" that would appear on his *Nashville Rebel* album that same year—1966—was haunting. Waylon sang with utter confidence. He approached the story boldly. You would have thought that John Lennon and Paul McCartney had custom-written the song to be sung by a wanderlust character like Waylon. I was mesmerized.

He worked quickly and efficiently, critiquing his vocals with cold objectivity. When he had a take he liked, he turned to Duane and said, "Well, let's hear that song your missus wrote."

I went to the piano and played the song one time through.

"Wow," said Waylon. "That little lady can really sing."

"And write," added Duane.

"Good song," Waylon continued. "Who sings the first verse—you or me?"

"Why don't you start off," I suggested.

"Don't mind if I do. But you ain't gonna reach the microphone without something to stand on. Lemme move this box over here."

Waylon sang:

> Once we were so in love
> We found the joy true love's made of
> I changed my mind, I set you free

How could I make such a mistake
I'll never see

Then, standing on the box, I sang:

I went my way, I lived with pain
I found your faith for love in vain
You came back, I turned away
I live each day regretting the way
We destroyed yesterday

"Whoa!" Waylon held up his hand to stop the engineer. "She's drowning me out. She's got more volume than me. I'd better move that box a few feet back from the mic."

With me repositioned, together we sang:

So here we are,
Living proof of what two fools in love can do
Someday we will,
But it's too late
We're living proof
There's nothing left of our yesterday

The harmony came naturally. During the playback, Waylon was grinning ear to ear.

"Have any other songs?" he asked.

"A bunch," I said, "but not ready to play for you tonight. You've got your album to record."

"Well, don't forget me when you start shopping those songs around."

"I won't," I promised.

He and Duane had a good, hearty handshake before we walked out. While I was leaving, I turned around to see if Waylon was looking at me. He was. Our eyes met and if eyes could talk, Lord only knows what they would have said at that moment.

I look back now at the story of that song and wonder what was going through my mind when I sang it with Waylon. At the time, we were both married. Later I'd learn that he was as unhappy in his marriage as I was in mine, but there was no lengthy personal talk during that first encounter, only singing. Ironically, the song was about a marriage gone bad, living with pain, and dealing with the results of a ruined relationship. I was not consciously telling the story of my own marriage. But writers, especially ones like me, are always unknowingly dipping into the dark recesses of their minds for material.

My subconscious contained a lot more sadness than my surface personality—the ebullient demeanor I've had since childhood—was willing to reveal. My surface personality wanted the world to see that everything was all right, that as a wife, mother, and songwriter, I was making do.

But I was hurting inside. I'm not sure how much my flirtation with Ayn Rand's theories of self-obsession had affected me. I now know that it didn't help. It also didn't help that, given my state of disbelief, I chose not to turn to God for comfort. Instead, I suffered silently.

There came a time when it no longer made sense to keep suffering. A decision had to be made. Clearly, I couldn't see myself staying in a marriage characterized not only by the absence of romantic love but by an alarming increase in acrimony. Drained of compassion, I could no longer abide Duane's jealousy. Nor could I go through the paces—and the pretense—of a normal life. I was tired of feeling trapped in the golden ghetto of Beverly Hills, tired of the manicured man-made landscape of Southern California, tired of hiding my hopelessness. Rather than risk an escalation of bad feelings between Duane and me, I decided to cut the cord.

Emotionally, divorce is an ugly business. How can it be otherwise? Divorce is an admission no one wants to make. Divorce can also provoke bad behavior—rage and revenge. Knowing that and loving our daughter as we did, Duane and I made an effort to avoid rancor and to stay civil. I credit him for doing just that. Since I was not interested in anything but the most modest of settlements, there were no arguments over money. All I required was some child support for Jennifer.

Through the years, Duane and I remained on cordial terms. He adored our daughter and remained in her life. During the pre-divorce separation period, I took Jennifer and shared an apartment with Shelley Fabares, who had left Lou Adler. We lived there for a short while until my brother Johnny flew out from Arizona. He helped pack us up and drove us home in my '64 Mustang. I say "home" because, try as I might, Los Angeles never felt like home.

I still saw Mesa as my home and yet, after this long and difficult absence, wondered what it would be like to return to the fold of my family. I had left when I was eighteen. Now I was twenty-four. Now I was a divorcee and the mother of a small child. What lay ahead?

— Part Two —

THE LIGHTNING

---------------- Chapter 9 ----------------

WAYLON AT JD'S

BEFORE WAYLON, I SAW MYSELF LIVING ON A CLOUD.

After Waylon, lightning struck—and kept striking for thirty-three years.

I first felt the lightning in 1968 when my sister Sharon suggested that we go see Waylon at JD's, the outsized two-story nightclub where he'd been the big star since 1964.

I was back home. Jennifer and I were living with my folks who welcomed me home with open arms. They had no questions about why or how my marriage had ended. They understood me well enough to sense how unhappy I had been. And they trusted me enough to know that I would never take divorce lightly. They saw that my decision came after years of struggle.

Religion was not discussed. Here, too, Mother's sensitivity told her that words would be in vain. She never demanded that I attend her church. She left me to my own spiritual devices, or lack thereof. Between us were unspoken volumes of dialogue about the true nature of God. Were that dialogue spoken, we both feared the results. Neither of us wanted to bring acrimony to our relationship. Thus, on matters of the spirit, the silence endured.

My sister Sharon reentered my story in her typically irrepressible way. Just as she was the one who initially urged me to meet Duane, she was one of the key catalysts in getting me out of the house to see Waylon.

"I've heard him many times," she said. "I've even met him before JD's when he used to play at Wild Bill's. That's when I heard all about his wild side. But who cares? I'm telling you, Mirriam, this Waylon Jennings is one of the best singers, one of the best entertainers out there. Since he's already sung a song with you, I'm sure he'd love to see you again. What do you say?"

What could I say? I remembered the look that he and I had exchanged when I left the studio a year ago. I said yes.

Waylon was the king of Phoenix and JD's was his castle. His fans were fiercely loyal. He and his band, the Waylors, had become the stuff of legend. When his first RCA album *Folk-Country* came out, he curtailed his permanent residence at JD's in favor of touring to support the record. So when he did return to JD's for an occasional one-nighter, it was seen as a super-special occasion.

The night when Sharon and I went to see him was one such occasion. By that point I'd been to hundreds of live shows, both as performer and as fan. But I had never seen a scene like Waylon at JD's. The club, at 825 North Scottsdale Road, was a madhouse of music. There was a rocking band downstairs while on the second-story dance floor, big enough for twelve hundred screaming fans, Waylon had them packed in like sardines.

Waylon still maintained the clean-shaven look I'd seen a year earlier. He wore a western-style white shirt with black trim.

"Handsome devil, ain't he?" Sharon said as we moved toward the bandstand.

I couldn't argue with that. He looked great and sounded even better. The music was jolting, intoxicating, irresistible. He played everything from Chuck Berry's "Memphis, Tennessee" to Bob Dylan's

"Girl from the North Country" to Johnny Cash's "The Restless Kid" to his own "Just to Satisfy You." He sang with a natural and unrelenting force that gained momentum over his long set. The high-voltage energy generated by the crowd and the electric music made me feel as if I were floating on air.

"Look," said Sharon at one point, "he's pointing at you. He's wanting you to come up onstage."

Sharon was right. Waylon had spotted me and—just like that—was gesturing for me to join him. I was hesitant but he was insistent.

"Come on up," he said, "or I'm not gonna sing another note."

So I went.

"This little gal sure can sing," he told the crowd. "Wait till you hear her." Then, whispering in my ear, he asked, "You know 'It Ain't Me, Babe'?"

"The Bob Dylan song?"

"That's the one."

I loved Dylan—still do—and was glad he'd chosen that particular number, an easy song to sing.

I guess I held my own because the crowd responded with loud cheers. It turned out to be the last song of his set.

During the intermission, he stayed close to me and said, "Heard you and Duane split up."

"You heard right," I said.

"Well, then, how'd you like to run off with me?"

The statement startled me, frightened me, and, I have to confess, delighted me. It took me a second or two to rebound.

"Call me in six months," I said.

"Why six months?"

"I'm still recovering from my last marriage."

"That makes two of us. The next move is yours," Waylon added before saying good-bye.

On the way home Sharon was aflutter.

"You're going out with him, aren't you?" she said.

"No."

"But he asked you, didn't he?"

"In a manner of speaking."

"So what's the problem?" my sister wanted to know.

"I just got out of one difficult relationship and I'm not about to dive into another difficult one."

"Why do you call him difficult?"

"You were the one who called him wild."

"All these entertainers like fast living. That's what makes them so goshdarn fascinating. Don't care what you say, Mirriam, I think you're interested."

I didn't want to admit it then, but Sharon was right. I was deeply interested but also deeply apprehensive. The more people in Phoenix talked about Waylon, the more incorrigible he appeared. It wasn't only the long list of women he had supposedly seduced (or who had seduced him), it was also his reputation for being high on high-potency pep pills.

And yet . . .

I sensed something in this man that I couldn't ignore. I saw him as a fellow adventurer, a man unafraid of uncharted territory, someone willing to go anywhere and do anything in pursuit of some ever-elusive truth.

I couldn't get him off my mind. And just when I thought I had, I happened to turn on the TV and there he was. Unlike the night I saw him at JD's, he looked awful. He had lost considerable weight and, in his weird Nehru jacket, gave the impression of a man in pain. His face was gaunt and his eyes vacant. I couldn't help but worry about him. And, even more pointedly, I couldn't help thinking a thought that alarmed me:

He needs me.

I say the thought alarmed me because I questioned its validity. Who was I to help him? Who was I to presume he needed help?

I nonetheless acted on my instinct. I wrote him a letter in which I said that come Christmas season, which was still a few months away, I would be in Phoenix and if he was playing JD's I'd like to see him.

His answer came within days. He wanted to see me.

When the day arrived, I dressed up to look my best and, for comfort's sake, brought along my brother Johnny. Good thing, because Waylon left word to see him before the show at his suite at the Caravan Hotel. Highly apprehensive, I didn't want to arrive alone.

In his autobiography, Waylon recalled that he was shirtless when he greeted me. He said the room was in shambles, filled with smoke, his band in the middle of a hot poker game. My own memories are not all that clear. I suppose that my excitement at seeing Waylon again clouded the details. In any event, I'm certain that I was not shocked. I had seen disheveled musicians in messy hotel rooms before. I do remember that, with my brother seated between us, Waylon and I had a surprisingly intimate conversation.

I later learned that when Waylon liked someone, he couldn't help but speak intimately. Sincerity flowed out of him. He had no filter. He wasn't cagey or vague or duplicitous. Waylon Jennings was straight-ahead, a man who spoke his mind. He liked to laugh and laughed easily and often. He was a tease but used teasing as an expression of affection. If he was fond of you, he'd tease you. If he wasn't, he'd ignore you. But you couldn't ignore him. He was too bombastic to be ignored, too charismatic, too filled with fun and good-hearted mischief. Most of all, he was energy personified, supercharged, propulsive energy bottled up into a man whose chief outlet was dynamic music.

"I have to be making music," he was quick to tell me. "If I'm not singing it, I'm writing it. If I'm not writing it, I'm putting it together. And if I'm not putting it together, I'm going crazy. Music is what keeps me from going crazy."

About his personal life, he couldn't have been plainer. "I've gone through my three marriages like Grant going through Richmond."

Three marriages, I thought to myself, *and he's only thirty-one.*

My apprehension was still great, but my curiosity was even greater. My feelings were deeply conflicted: fear and attraction, caution and impetuosity. Being with Waylon was like being in a vortex over which I had no control. My head was spinning.

My head was spinning even faster when, after our talk in his hotel suite, I went to the show where the power of his music smashed the last remnants of my doubts. Yes, I wanted to see this man again—this man whose phenomenal two-hour set included wildly unique versions of songs by Roy Orbison, Willie Nelson, Mel Tillis, the Beatles, Buck Owens, and the Beach Boys. By the time the show was over, I was drained.

I wasn't sure what would happen next. But whatever it was, I couldn't wait.

Chapter 10

LOVE OF THE COMMON PEOPLE

BETWEEN OUR TALK AT THE CARAVAN HOTEL AND OUR FIRST encounter—a week or so later—I had time to consider the circumstances. Despite his reputation, Waylon had been a perfect gentleman, respectful to both my brother and me. I didn't detect the slightest sign of sexual aggression or overassertiveness. He was highly animated, but hardly predatory. He made me feel safe. And yet he could read my hesitancy.

"I know you've heard lots of bad stuff about me," he said, "but if I told you I actually considered studying for the ministry, would that help my case?"

"Wouldn't hurt. But you obviously changed your mind. What happened?"

"Long story. But something I could explain on our first date. What do you say?"

I said yes.

On that first date he invited me to another of his shows. He came by my folks' house and charmed them both. Waylon could charm anyone.

When we got into the car, he asked, "Mind if I call you Runt?"

"I can think of a few more flattering names."

"It's just that you're so little, and besides, 'Mirriam' sounds too formal."

"Well, let's dispense with formalities. Where are we going, by the way?"

"A long drive. You mind?"

"Depends on the destination."

"Tuba City."

"Okay."

"Don't you want to know why we're driving there?"

"I'm guessing 'cause the Navajos like your music. Tuba City is located in the Navajo Nation."

"Good guess. Ever since I put out that record called *Love of the Common People*, the Indians have really taken to my music. You heard that record?"

"I haven't."

"You need to."

"Do I really need to know all your records?"

"Don't see why not," he said with an endearingly devilish grin before asking, "Have you really been to Tuba City?"

"I'm an Arizona girl," I said. "I know my state."

I knew Tuba City, sitting in the Painted Desert on the western edge of the Navajo territory, as an area of stark and breathtaking beauty.

"I figured that this long drive," said Waylon, "will give us some time to chat."

"And if I run out of things to say?" I asked.

"Not to worry. I'll fill in the blanks."

Waylon did that—and then some. With unflinching candor, he spoke about the hardships of growing up in Littlefield, a tiny dot on the map of West Texas, thirty miles outside of Lubbock.

"Littlefield is on the caprock," he said, "right at the foot of the Great Plains as they stretch through Denver all the way north to Canada. Its elevation is about four thousand feet, but it's so flat your dog could run off and you could watch him go for three days."

He talked about growing up the oldest of four boys, dirt poor, and spending much of his childhood working the fields.

"Hard work—bone-crushing, skin-bleeding hard work—is all I've ever known," he said.

"Were your folks churchgoing people?" I asked.

"Church of God in Christ. Strict fundamentalists. The gospel I heard preached was all fire and brimstone and the certainty of going straight to hell if you didn't walk the straight and narrow. It was the gospel of fear that was stuffed down my throat. 'Fraid I don't have good feelings about that church. Of all the religions I've run into, I do believe the Church of Christ has it wronger than most."

"Why do you say that?"

"'Cause of what they taught me about God."

"And what's that?"

"According to what I learned in the Church of Christ, God is one angry dude who gave us this instruction book that's hard to understand. But that doesn't matter because, whether you understand it or not, you'd better obey every word. If you don't, you'll burn up in a lake of fire for all eternity. Yes, ma'am, that's what I was taught. So you can see why I don't love the church."

"If you feel that way, what made you want to study for the ministry?"

"Mama wanted one of her boys to be a preacher. I suppose I was trying to please her."

"But didn't get too far."

"Didn't get too far with any of my schooling."

"But you kept going to church," I said.

"Not for too long. Couldn't take it. What about you? You said your mom was a preacher. Wouldn't imagine being a preacher's kid you had much fun."

"You're wrong. I liked it."

"You did?"

"Sure did."

"You're gonna have to explain why."

I went on to speak about the beauty of Mother's church, about how love, and not fear, was the message. But I also admitted that I'd left my faith several years back. Waylon wanted to know why.

"Not sure. I guess it's because I've been busy exploring other ways of looking at the world."

"And what did you find?"

"Only that I need to keep exploring," I said.

"Makes sense to me. I'm not sure the exploring stops until the day we die."

"Which may be the day that the real exploring just begins."

"I like how you think," he said with a broad smile.

A little later up the road a horse came out of nowhere and Waylon, who turned the wheel just in time to avoid the animal, started laughing.

"What's so doggone funny?" I wanted to know.

"The peaceful look on that horse's face. He wasn't scared in the least. These animals know how to live. It's thinking that makes humans nuts."

"Do you include yourself in that group of nutty humans?" I asked.

"I'm the leader of that group."

As the leader of his music group, the Waylors, Waylon held that audience of Native Americans spellbound. It was a magical night.

Unlike the raucous crowd at JD's, this was an audience that showed restraint—a restraint born out of respect and reverence. The Navajos seemed to connect to the deepest part of Waylon's soul. There was a sadness in his songs I hadn't heard before. These people, his devoted fans, were moved by an ever-present tear in his voice, a sense of loss and pain that sat in the center of his songs. They loved him.

"The Navajos call it the long walk," said Waylon on the drive back to Mesa. "They were forced off their land into exile. The government marched them to eastern New Mexico and tried turning them into farmers and traders, contrary to their hunting and shepherding ways. Took years for America to admit its mistake and send them home to this land they call the Wondrous Place. Anyway, they make me feel like I belong."

"I felt a sadness in your voice tonight I hadn't heard before."

"Probably 'cause I was thinking about my daddy. I lost him earlier this year."

"I'm so sorry."

"He was only fifty-one. Bad ticker. Beautiful man. Most decent man I've ever known. And the hardest worker to boot."

"What did he do for a living?" I asked as we drove through the dark, moonlit desert on our way back to Mesa.

"What didn't he do? At one time or another, he worked the fields, ran a creamery, owned a produce store, had a gas station, and drove a fuel truck. Never did make much money but none of us starved. Never will forget the time he went to Hobbs, New Mexico, to do construction work and a piece of lumber fell on him. Daddy got out of the hospital in a back brace and headed right out to the cotton fields. 'Why are you doing that?' Mama asked him. ' 'Cause it's cotton-picking time, and I can't afford not to.'"

"He must have been proud of you."

"He was. He loved music and appreciated musicians. He played guitar in that thumb-and-finger plucking style used by Jimmie Rodgers and Mother Maybelle Carter. His idol was Bill Monroe. On a clear night, messing with the booster cables, he'd hook up the radio so we could pull in the *Louisiana Hayride* or the *Grand Ole Opry*. That's when I first heard Hank Williams sing 'Lost Highway.' Even had a premonition about Hank. I was in the general store in Littlefield and 'I'll Never Get Out of Here Alive' came over the radio. I thought to myself, *Wouldn't it be weird if he died?* Well, he did. That very day. New Year's Day, 1953. He was twenty-nine. I was fifteen. And it tore me up, almost like my daddy had died."

"Duane told me that you were with Buddy Holly on the night that he died," I said. "That must have been so hard for you."

"Still is," Waylon acknowledged. "Buddy was one of the first to believe in me. He put me in his band on bass even though I really didn't know the bass. Talk about being scared! But I hung in 'cause I knew Buddy was a genius. He was everything I loved—rock and roll and country and western and rhythm and blues, all packed into one incredible artist. When I was a deejay in Lubbock, Buddy's hometown, he was my idol. To go on tour with him was a dream come true. And then that godawful night . . ."

Waylon was struck silent. Seconds ticked by.

"You don't need to talk about it . . ."

"I do need to talk about it. For years I couldn't. For years it haunted me. For years I felt guilty. Later I learned they even have a name for it—survivor's guilt. For years I was messed up behind the memory. The memory is as clear today as it was on February 3, 1959. You gotta remember—he was only twenty-two, I was twenty-one. We were at that age when you think you're gonna live forever."

Waylon went on to describe the fateful tour that featured Buddy Holly, Ritchie Valens, and the Big Bopper, J. P. Richardson. They were traveling on an old bus with a broken heater. After their show in Clear Lake, Iowa, they were due to drive all night to Moorhead, Minnesota. That's when Buddy decided to charter a small plane that seated only three passengers. The original plan was that Waylon and guitarist Tommy Allsup would fly with Buddy. But the Big Bopper, down with the flu, was reluctant to ride on the freezing bus and asked Waylon to relinquish his seat. Out of compassion, bighearted Waylon agreed. Ritchie Valens also preferred to fly and, after winning a coin toss with Allsup, secured the third seat.

At the end of the night, Buddy said to Waylon, "Heard you're not flying with me tonight. You chicken out?"

"Are you kidding? I ain't scared of flying. Just trying to be a good guy and let the Big Bopper take my seat."

"Well," said Buddy, "I hope your bus freezes up again."

"And I hope your ol' plane crashes."

Buddy, Ritchie, and the Big Bopper flew into a raging storm while Waylon and Allsup rode the all-night bus. Waylon said that he slept like a baby. He didn't learn about the plane crash until he arrived in Moorhead the next morning. Back in his hometown of Littlefield, his parents heard a news report that Buddy Holly and his band were all dead. For nearly a whole day they thought they'd lost their son.

"Such a tragic story," I said.

"I can't tell you how many years I thought that, in some twisted way, I'd caused it. Sometimes I still have nightmares about it. And Buddy—I can't tell you how much I loved that guy, how much he meant to me. He wrote some of the greatest songs of the century before he was twenty-one. Can you imagine what he would have written if he'd lived even to middle age? It's such a loss."

"Yet we haven't lost his music. His music sounds better than ever. It'll never get stale, just as Buddy will stay forever young," I said.

"Tell me about the music you loved when you were young," said Waylon. "What's the first music that caught your fancy?"

"Music I learned in Mother's church. Music I played. Music I sang."

"But music that didn't stick with you," said Waylon.

"I wouldn't say that. I loved the music. Still do."

"Maybe that music is just on pause," said Waylon.

"That's a nice way of putting it."

"I'm trying to show you I'm a nice guy."

"Your dad must have been a nice guy. You were talking about him before you brought up Buddy. Tell me more about your father."

"Most important thing about Daddy is that it was him, not the church, who taught me right from wrong. It was him who protected me. Once, a stud named Strawberry, a huge beefy boxer and the local Golden Gloves heavyweight champ, was about to beat up my little brother Tommy. Seems as though Tommy had fought with Strawberry's little brother. Daddy found out and stepped in between Strawberry and Tommy. 'You don't want to mess with me,' said Strawberry. 'I'm undefeated.' 'You may be undefeated,' said Daddy, 'but lay one hand on my son and I'll break you in half.' That stone-cold-killer look Daddy gave Strawberry has stayed with me all my life. Strawberry just turned around and walked away. That's when I realized my dad was the best protection any boy could ever have."

"That's a heavy statement, Waylon."

"I have a heavy heart. Without Daddy, I don't think I'll ever feel safe again."

I didn't know what to say so I stayed silent. Outside the black sky was sprinkled with stars. Waylon was focused on the highway ahead. I could sense that he was still thinking about his father. His eyes grew moist. Tears fell. I took his hand and held it.

Chapter 11

RHYTHMS

EVERY RELATIONSHIP HAS A RHYTHM. SOME DEVELOP TENTA-tively, speed up, and then slow down to a drag. Others start off at a frantic pace before quickly running out of steam. There are relation-ships that maintain an even rhythm for decades. And then there are those that are always losing the beat and falling out of sync.

The rhythm of the relationship I began to forge with Waylon seemed to contain a power all its own. I felt swept up, and I know Waylon felt the same. We were propelled by a force that neither of us had ever expe-rienced before. That force, of course, was love. I loved sitting next to him as we drove through Arizona from gig to gig. I loved watching him sing. Loved watching him play. Loved how he led his band. How he interacted with his fans. How he smiled. How he frowned. How he laughed. How he cried. How he spoke. How he stayed silent. I loved how sincerity directed his every thought, his every move, his every moment.

I loved this man and everything—

I was about to write "and everything about him," but I've stopped myself in time. In the aftermath of meeting Waylon, I might well have said those words. I was blissed out, starry-eyed in love. I realized that this would not be a conventional relationship because he was not a conventional man. I knew I was in for a wild ride. There could be no doubt that Waylon was a wild man.

I also knew—and this is the part that prevents me from writing "I loved everything about him"—that he had a habit. As he himself readily confessed, he was addicted to amphetamines. Sometimes he called them diet pills or pep pills or any number of colorful nicknames like Speckled Birds, Little Bitty Desoxyns, Desbuton Pancakes, or more personal handles like Waylon's Phoenix Flashes. He called LA Turnarounds the most effective because, as he said, "you could take one and drive to Los Angeles, turn around, and come straight back."

He carefully avoided detailing his drug habit to me. "I never liked downers," he wrote in his autobiography. "I was hyper and taking uppers on top of that. I never hit the ground for decades to come. I had incredible stamina; I prided myself on the fact that I could take more pills, stay up longer, sing more songs, and love on more women than most anybody you ever met in your life. I didn't know when to stop, or see any need to."[1]

He also wrote about being caught up in a culture—the music business culture—where washing down a handful of pills was as normal as drinking a beer. Not that he gave excuses. Waylon wasn't one to rationalize. He did what he did because he wanted to do it. My presumption then—and now—is that his main motivation for pill-popping was to simply stay up. That may sound simplistic, but I believe it with all my heart. Life excited him to such an extent that he didn't want to sleep. He didn't want to miss a thing. And the part of life that excited him most was creativity. He wanted to compose music, play music, arrange music, and record music every minute of every day. If pills helped prolong his energy and kept him going long into the night and well into the morning, then he wasn't about to resist.

I couldn't resist Waylon if I tried. And, believe me, I did try. I tried to tell myself that his lifestyle was too bizarre, too risky, too uncertain. I certainly saw that he had a serious relationship with pills, yet I didn't see—at least not at first—how that relationship would negatively impact me. Yes, he was high, but his high seemed no different than my high, which is a natural high. It was a high with a positive slant, a high that said I'm doing all I can to live life to the fullest.

Beneath the high—this ongoing explosion of inexhaustible energy—was a soul I saw as sensitive, sweet, and fundamentally good. Waylon dealt with the world—and everyone in it—squarely and fairly. His word was his bond. Not for a second did I ever doubt his fundamental integrity.

Our love was deeply spiritual, but also powerfully physical. For the first time in my life, I understood the meaning of the old standard song that talked about loving a man body and soul. Sexual satisfaction, combined with romantic intoxication, made for a heady brew. I didn't want to be separated from this man—not for a minute.

Yet, the rhythm of our romance got disrupted early on. The first instance was a recording date Waylon had in Nashville. I stayed behind in Phoenix with Jennifer at my sister Sharon's house. Waylon said he'd be back in a few days.

A few days became many days. Many days became many weeks. And still no Waylon. He flat-out disappeared. No letters, no calls. I had no idea where he was.

"I'll find him," said Sharon, seeing how upset I was.

"How are you going to do that?"

"Leave it to me. I'll chase him down."

It didn't take Sharon long. She was a woman with an enormous network of people. Critical contacts were her specialty. After a few hours on the phone, she'd located him.

"He's going to call you," said Sharon.

"When?" I asked.

"Soon."

Soon involved another two days of waiting. By the time he did call, I was infuriated.

"Got in a jam," he said. "And it took a while to work things out. But I'll be home soon and I just want you to know that nothing has changed. I still love you, baby. I love you more than ever."

"That's good to hear," I said, "but what am I supposed to make of this disappearing act?"

"Doesn't amount to a thing. See you in a few days."

Sharon learned the story that Waylon would later confirm. While working in Nashville, he had slept with one of the female singers on his recording date. He saw it as a one-night affair. She saw it as much more. A few days later, she arrived at Waylon's hotel with her four children in tow. She had left her husband for Waylon. Waylon didn't want any part of it. But the woman wouldn't be dissuaded. She wouldn't budge. Meanwhile, her husband was incensed. He grabbed his gun and told anyone who'd listen that Waylon was as good as dead. When Waylon got wind of the man's mission, he had to go into hiding until cooler heads prevailed. The drama played out over weeks.

Such information would be enough for a levelheaded woman to call the whole thing off. I considered that idea. But, when it came to loving Waylon, I was hardly levelheaded. I gave him a hard time when he finally showed up, but ultimately I capitulated. My relationship to Waylon and his sometimes wandering ways was complicated. Yes, I was tolerant. And yes, I gave him wide latitude. At the same time, I did my fair share of suffering and, as you will soon see, there were times when I bolted.

Paradoxically, though, I wouldn't characterize our relationship as volatile. We never had knock-down-drag-out fights. We didn't throw plates at each other. We never even slammed doors. There was never the slightest hint of violence. We had a wordless way of dancing around each other's moods. The chemistry between us was as natural as it was inexplicable. Instinctively we knew how to navigate the tricky waters that sometimes separated us. Neither of us lived in the past or the future. We were planted in present tense. And because we were in the moment, we understood that any particular moment, particularly the uncomfortable ones, would soon pass.

When I did hit a rough patch, I had resources that helped me deal with negative emotions. My chief resource was music. I deeply believe that music was a key element to my surviving these early years with Waylon. Were I not a writer, I'm not sure I would have been able to process the mess of contradictory emotions invading my heart. In taking my tangle of feelings—anger, fear, confusion—and giving them a musical voice, I managed to work myself out of a state of rage. The rage remained in the songs.

An example is "It's All Over Now," written during this time when I was trying to cope with this incorrigible creature. The story is not literal. None of my songs are exact slices of my life. I take poetic license in framing the scene. But the emotions are real. The emotions are mine.

> When I was loving you, I gave all I had to give
> You took that love I gave, you took my will to live
> You didn't want me then, babe, what
> > brings you back in now
> I hear you talking, but just keep walking,
> It's all over now
> How does it feel to be on the other side
> Drop down to your knees, naked of your pride
> Maybe next time you'll know what you're looking for
> Maybe you can give her all she needs and more
> You didn't have the love I needed, I don't need it now

The great irony is when I played "It's All Over Now" for Waylon, he not only understood it, he loved it. He praised me to the sky. At first I thought his praise was just a way to get him off the hook. But it wasn't. He was genuine.

"The way you put all those feelings in your song," he said, "and the way you sing it—women all over the world will relate."

No doubt, Waylon's support of my music was a huge factor in repairing our relationship. He became my biggest booster. Convinced that I had been under-recorded or wrongly recorded, he was dead set on correcting that. He thought I needed to get out there onstage, front and center.

"You've been like a bird in a gilded cage," he said. "We need to open the cage door and let the bird fly free."

Such words were deeply reassuring, not because I longed to be a star but because my years as a semi-secluded Beverly Hills housewife had frustrated my inner artist. It wasn't enough to have a few of my songs covered by other singers. I felt the need to sing them myself.

I sometimes wonder how I would have reacted had my parents discouraged me from staying with Waylon. After all, he was an untamed, hard-living rock-and-roll country star. He might have appeared to be just the kind of guy they wouldn't want their beloved daughter to date. Yet the truth is that both Mother and Daddy adored Waylon. And he adored them.

An adventurer himself, Waylon recognized and respected that audacious spirit in my parents. Waylon saw that Arnold Johnson possessed the indomitable personality of a Wild West prospector. He admired my father's dazzling scientific mind and knowledge of all things mechanical.

At first Waylon may have worried that Mother might proselytize and bring back bad memories of his childhood church. But Mother instinctively understood that sermonizing would only estrange him. Instead, she gave him wide berth. She had too much integrity to hide her religious convictions, but too much wisdom to flaunt them. In no uncertain terms, she let Waylon know that she loved him and soon came to see him as a son, a son who reminded her of Paul, who had died at such a young age. Sensing Waylon's devotion to me, she never failed to support us even during our dark days.

One of the darkest days happened in the early seventies when Waylon was playing Panther Hall in Fort Worth. After the show a gaggle of girls, practically falling out of their clothes, came up to him, while I was standing right there. The tallest one got right in his face and said, "Hey, Waylon, do you wanna f___?"

I was shocked. Waylon wasn't. I had never heard young women speak this way. Waylon had. He just laughed and let them pass.

When we were back in my dressing room, I was rattled. Playing shows with Duane, I'd seen willing women, but nothing this brazen.

"Happens all the time," said Waylon. "We even have a name for it."

"I'm not sure I want to know."

"Sure you do. They're the Whore Core."

"Except they're not charging."

"One way or another, you wind up paying a pretty price."

"So this is just life on the road with Waylon Jennings."

"'Fraid so."

With Waylon, things just happened. Things just flowed. To go with the flow was easy. To resist it was hard. And yet, as I surrendered to the rhythm of our romance, anxiety cropped up. Nagging doubts came late at night or first thing in the morning. Why was I charging ahead? Why was I throwing caution to the wind? What was I getting myself into? I'd already seen how this man's behavior was anything but predictable. Didn't I need to slow down? Didn't I need to take a deep breath and reconsider the situation? Didn't I need to get out before it was too late?

After all was said and done, knowing what I knew and seeing what I saw, did I really truly want to spend the rest of my life with this man?

The answer was yes.

Chapter 12

"YOU WANNA GET MARRIED, DON'T YOU?"

WAYLON POPPED THE QUESTION AFTER DATING ME FOR LESS than a year.

For several long seconds, I stayed silent.

"Just like that?" I finally asked.

"Just like that."

"You sure?" I asked again.

"I'm sure I love you. And I'm sure that's enough. You have doubts?"

"You know I do," I said.

"Well, that's only reason to love you more. You're honest about your doubts. But if I know you—and I think I do—you won't let those doubts stop you. So just say yes and let's get on with it."

I said yes and we got on with it.

To be truthful, his proposal didn't come as a surprise. I saw it coming months before. In fact, ever since I'd gone out on the road with Waylon, I'd been packing a wedding dress—nothing fancy, mind you, but a suitable outfit.

Yet the fact that I was prepared sartorially doesn't mean that I was prepared emotionally. I was still scared of what permanent residence in the world of Waylon would look like—so scared that I spent most of our wedding day—October 26, 1969—nervously laughing.

I laughed when we got to the Las Vegas City Hall. I laughed when Waylon's best man turned out to be his bass player who hit the same wrong notes every night and whose chief job was to carry the money briefcase. I laughed when the justice of the peace, whose deadly monotone that gave the impression that this was his hundredth wedding of the day, called me Mary instead of Mirriam. I laughed when I saw Waylon taking the ceremony super seriously. I laughed when I looked around and saw I had no bridesmaid in attendance, no parents, no family at all. I even laughed when I was supposed to say, "I do." I laughed because I was nervous and scared and convinced that this was either the best day of my life or the worst. I laughed because I saw myself going on a ride with no turning back. I laughed because I didn't know what else to do.

We could have waited. We could have planned. We could have arranged a big wedding with his mom and my mom and everyone who meant the most to us. But Waylon didn't want to wait and, in the end, neither did I. It felt more like an elopement than a thought-out marriage.

After the ceremony, we wound up at the Golden Nugget for a champagne dinner. The champagne only made me laugh harder.

"This ain't no laughing matter," said Waylon, who was all laughed out.

"If I don't laugh," I said, "I'll cry."

"Cries of regret or cries of joy?" he asked.

"Both."

"For crying out loud, girl, just admit it. There ain't no one in this whole dang world you'd rather marry than me."

"I admit it, but I'm still laughing about it."

We moved to Nashville for obvious reasons. Nashville was Music Center, headquarters for RCA's country music division. Nashville was home to Chet Atkins, Waylon's producer and a great supporter of my music. Nashville was centrally located, a logical point of departure for our nonstop road treks.

Waylon had history in Nashville. A few years before we met, he'd gone there to record for RCA under Chet Atkins's supervision. That was a wild period when Waylon shared an apartment with Johnny Cash. Waylon told hilarious stories of Johnny's inept but valiant attempts to bake biscuits, his face covered with white flour. They had more in common besides a love of music. They both loved popping pills. While they knew that the other one was indulging, Waylon said that they never shared their stash. They never even mentioned their mutual habit.

They were the Odd Couple, running around town like teenage boys, going for days without sleep. It was in Nashville that they forged a friendship that lasted a lifetime. That friendship, however, was somewhat remote when I came on the scene. Johnny's wife June was apprehensive about her husband's bond with Waylon, whom she considered a bad influence. June kept Johnny on a short leash and wasn't at all eager for the two men to socialize. It took a number of years for June to relax and allow the two men to renew their friendship.

Waylon decided to head for Nashville and set up shop. I was amenable. We found a nice condo on West End, the first of our many rental abodes. Seems like we were moving every eight or nine months.

The period following our marriage was hectic, exciting, creative, and disturbing. So much was happening at once. Waylon proved to be a wonderfully caring father to Jennifer. And when, given the serious problems he was having with his former wife Maxine, he asked whether I'd object to our taking in their three children—Buddy, ten; Julie, eleven; and Terry, thirteen—I readily agreed. I wanted to do all I could to make Waylon's life manageable.

Blending the two families was not easy. I made the mistake of trying to be a friend to Waylon's kids when, in fact, they required a disciplinarian. Knowing they had been neglected, I tried to heal their hurt with kindness. My approach, no matter how well-meaning, didn't work. Strict boundaries would have given them a sense of security, but I lacked that insight. In that regard, I'm afraid I failed them.

Management was always a problem. For years, W. E. "Lucky" Moeller had been Waylon's manager and booker. Combining both roles ultimately proved problematic. Waylon saw Lucky as a father figure. When Waylon's father died, he grew even more dependent on Lucky. At the same time, Waylon understood how Lucky was working both sides of the street, often to the artist's disadvantage.

Lucky was an old-school promoter who'd booked everyone, beginning in the forties with Bob Wills. In addition to promoting, he also ran nightclubs and dance halls where he'd feature his artists like Webb Pierce and Kitty Wells, whom he called his White Horses. Lucky was in the two-sided position of both paying for and selling talent. Sometimes that worked against Waylon. When, for example, Kitty would turn down a lowball offer from a club owner, he'd send in Waylon as a replacement at half Waylon's normal rate. One way or the other, though, Lucky kept Waylon working. But at the end of a long tour the numbers didn't add up.

"I love Lucky," said Waylon, "but after ten months on the road, I'd have to ask him, 'Hoss, how is it that I come to owe you thirty thousand dollars?'"

"What's his answer?" I asked Waylon.

"He just laughs and says, 'Look, son, I've always kept you working, and always will.'"

I understood the bond between Waylon and Lucky. But I also saw that, in addition to being a bond, it was a form of bondage. Because he didn't want to focus on the minutiae of managing his own money, Waylon turned over the task to someone who had a daddy-like dominance over him. I was alarmed by the implications of their relationship. But I was also aware of my own limitations. No matter how dysfunctional it might be, I knew better than to get into the middle of that long-term friendship. Thus the leak in Waylon's financial ship went unattended. It would take several more years before that leak got plugged.

Financial disorder is always disturbing. That disturbance was allayed, though, by all the excitement of the creative whirlwind in which we found ourselves. Waylon was in the studio making incredible albums like *Singer of Sad Songs* with killer versions of George Jones's "Ragged but Right" and the Rolling Stones' "Honky Tonk Women."

I was in the studio as well. In 1970, Chet Atkins finally decided that I was more than a songwriter. He now saw me as a solo artist and signed me to RCA. He and Waylon coproduced the album and were confident enough to call it *A Country Star Is Born*, a title that both excited and embarrassed me.

When the record was complete, Chet called me to his office. He said he had something important to discuss.

"Are you happy with the professional names you've used previously?"

"No," I said. "Mirriam Eddy is over, and Mirriam Johnson is too long. Besides, neither one sounds entertaining."

"Well, can you think of something else?"

I thought back to a story I once heard my father tell about Jesse James's chief counterfeiter. I remembered the man was called Jesse Colter. When I mentioned the name to Chet, he broke out into a smile.

"That's it!" he said.

"It is?"

"It's catchy, it's edgy, it's quirky. I do believe it's you."

I wrote it down on a piece of paper, changing Jesse to Jessi. I stared at it for a few seconds.

"Not bad," I said. "Not bad at all."

Chapter 13

THE BIRTH OF JESSI COLTER

WAYLON, WHO ALWAYS HAD A HARD TIME CALLING ME Mirriam, took to Jessi immediately. He agreed with Chet.

"You're a pistol," he said. "The name fits."

My mother didn't mind, but Daddy initially had problems.

"Jessi Colter doesn't represent the proudest moment in American history," he said, shaking his head. "Besides, it's a man's name."

I didn't reply. Daddy wasn't the type you talked back to. Eventually, though, he withdrew his complaint. Soon everyone, save my family—to whom I'll always be Mirriam—was calling me Jessi. I didn't mind. I didn't treat the changeover all that seriously. If Chet and RCA thought it would help sales, why not? If the name pleased my producer and my husband, I had no problem. Besides, it did have an adventuresome edge. I adopted it without further thought.

I did, however, devote enormous thought to the music I was making. This was, after all, my debut album. In the past I had recorded singles and saw this as a chance to stretch out and express the feelings that had been populating my heart. Those feelings came out in my songs. As a writer, I could never edit my emotions. So if you look at the underpinnings of the songs I wrote and performed on the record, you have some idea of what I was going through in my life.

My relationship with Waylon was still new. And even though he showered me with love and lavishly praised my music, he wasn't always there. He could disappear for days at a time. I knew Waylon loved women and their attention. He instinctively knew how to tease, flirt, and cause the heart to flutter.

Because neither one of us was confrontational, we avoided discussions of what he did when I was not around. He had made it clear from the start that my choice was to accept him as he was or not accept him at all.

"Don't try to remake me, Jessi," he had said. "It just won't work."

I lived with both the calming certainty of his love and the distressing uncertainty of his fidelity.

For my part, I loved the man inordinately. I loved his heart, his soul, and his stupendous artistry. I knew that deep down he was good as gold. But I also knew that his imperfections—his get-high propensities, his wandering eye—were making me a little crazy. The only way to cope with my craziness was to channel it into song.

"Songs," said Waylon, "are things you have to write. You can't ever stop writing songs."

One of the wonderful things about living with Waylon was my indoctrination into his wildly creative songwriting world. Harlan Howard said that Nashville in the sixties and seventies was like Paris in the twenties and thirties. Where the Lost Generation had Ernest Hemingway and F. Scott Fitzgerald, we had—just to name a few— Roger Miller, Tony Joe White, Willie Nelson, Johnny Cash, and a young man who came ramblin' through named Kris Kristofferson.

While the actual writing was done in private, the pullin' session was a community phenomenon. That's when the tunesmiths would come together—sometimes at the Holiday Inn on Nineteenth Street or at parties hosted by characters like Harlan Howard and Bobby Bare— and play their songs for one another.

While I was never intimidated, I was always inspired. They were powerful poets and dedicated craftsmen. They loved kidding around and putting each other on, but when it came to sculpting songs, they were dead serious. And don't think they weren't competitive. At the same time, the competition, though intense, was more good-hearted than ruthless. As an artistic community, these guys had a macho way of supporting and even nourishing one another.

While they wrote their stories of drinking and gambling, losing and winning, I wrote my own stories. I wrote songs that, through melody and metaphors, expressed my emotional ups and downs. Ironically, I sang the song that most clearly expressed my ambivalence about Waylon as a duet with Waylon! I called it "I Ain't the One." Read between the lines and you can sense what I was feeling about the uncertainty of our romance:

I sang:

> If you're looking for someone who's got it all to give
> Looking for someone who won't care how you live
> Looking for someone who don't need love from you
> I ain't the one, I ain't the one

Waylon sang:

> If you're looking for someone to dry
>   your tears when you cry
> Looking for someone to turn his back each time you lie
> Looking for someone to walk on and then walk by
> I ain't the one, I ain't the one

The story underscores a couple's refusal to tolerate anything short of uncompromised fidelity. That certainly was an attitude I wanted us to adopt, and when we sang the song—which turned into a fan favorite—we were convincing.

But how convinced was I? Uncertainty kept creeping into my mind. Scenarios kept me awake late at night. During one of those nights I wrote the song "If She's Where You Like Livin'":

> If she's where you like livin'
> You won't feel at home with me
> She tells you lies lookin' into your eyes
> She laughs but you don't see
> She knows just how to make you bow
> And you fall down on your knees
> How could such a man be crushed in her hand
> I don't believe I see

The most emotionally raw moment came when, without the camouflage of a complex story line, I simply cried, "Don't Let Him Go."

> Don't let him go
> Stop him if you can
> Don't let him go
> If you call him your man
> You didn't like something he did
> Could it be you've been wronged?
> Don't you know, woman, without your man
> You won't be a woman for long

Given the feminist tenor of the times—a feministic movement that resonated with me—you could view "Don't Let Him Go," the most mournful song I'd written up to that point, as anti-feminist. Wasn't the song basically saying that a woman is nothing without her man? Wasn't I saying that a woman's job is to accept her man, even if he has wronged her?

I made no apology for the song then, and I make none now. I didn't see the song in terms of what I was saying. I saw in terms of what I was feeling. My feelings didn't amount to any broad statement on feminism. My feelings were my own. They were fleeting. They were true—painfully true—at the moment I wrote the song. I put myself in the place of a woman who was on the verge of letting her man go. That woman could have easily been me. Part of me cried out, "Let him go!"

When those feelings swept over me, I wrote songs like "It's All Over Now," "I Ain't the One," and "If She's Where You Like Livin'." But those feelings passed and were replaced by others. One of those other feelings was fear—fear of losing someone I loved with all my heart, fear of giving up too soon, too impetuously, too impatiently. That feeling said to me, "Don't let him go. Hang in. Hang on. It's bound to get better."

As it turned out, I wrote only five of the eleven cuts on *A Country Star Is Born*. Chet wanted to supplement my output with tunes written by prominent country composers like Mickey Newbury, Harlan Howard, and Willie Nelson. In fact, if I had to choose my favorite song on the record, it might be Willie's haunting "Healing Hands of Time." Healing hands that "lead me safely through the night" seemed to be the perfect metaphor for the spirit I was seeking. Though I might not have admitted it at the time, my spirit required repair. I needed healing.

Part Three

THE RETURN

Chapter 14

OH WELL, THERE'S ALWAYS GOD

IF I HAD TO NAME A SONG THAT SPOKE MOST DIRECTLY TO MY soul during the turbulent early seventies, it wouldn't be one of mine or even one of Waylon's. It would be Harry Nilsson's version of "Without You," written by Badfinger's Peter Ham and Tom Evans.

That song possessed me, obsessed me, and somehow got me through a storm of confusion. Every time I heard it, I was able to access a sense of hope. Even though it's a sad song—or perhaps precisely because it's a sad song—hearing it lifted my heart. I believe great songs are transformative.

By virtue of the power of their melody and message, great songs turn sorrow to joy. The sheer joy of their soaring beauty cannot be resisted. And, at least in the moment we give ourselves over to the song, we are released from our pain and made to feel something positive.

Songs are ambiguous. Despite the writer's intention, they mean different things to different people. Often we don't even understand what they mean to us until, with the passage of time, we can look back and in a moment of clarity finally understand the significance.

On the surface, "Without You" is the simple story of someone who regrets letting a lover leave. It became a number-one pop hit for many weeks. Every time I heard it, I found myself holding back tears. It tore me up. For a while I thought that it was because in some ways it mirrored my anguish over Waylon and his inability to completely reform and his tendency to disappear unaccountably for days at a time. But now I've come to understand that the power of the song operated on a deeper level. Though I wasn't entirely conscious of it at the time, "Without You" spoke to that part of me that was without God.

My forays into non-Christian disciplines had gone nowhere. No philosophy had satisfied me. New Age formulations failed to work any magic in my mind. Objectivism fell by the wayside. Agnosticism left me longing. I was tired of reading convoluted tracts of theology. I was weary of exploring psychological principles of self-strength and self-dependence. When it came to considering theories of human behavior, I was spent.

Waylon saw this first. He knew I was looking for something I'd lost, but not possessing that "something" himself, he couldn't help me. Mother, of course, had seen my dilemma. But long ago she had decided that she wasn't the one who could bring me back. Only God could do that.

The four kids, Waylon, and I had moved to a home on Donelson Hills Drive in the Sunny Acres section of Nashville close to the Cumberland River. It was an ordinary afternoon. Waylon and I were planning to head out on the road in a few days, and I was making preparations. Waylon was working at the recording studio. The children were at school. I was walking down the stairs to our finished basement to search for something. I can't remember what I was looking for, but I do remember that the ceiling over the staircase was low—so low that if Waylon didn't bend down, he'd hit his head. I didn't have that problem. I was halfway down the stairs when a thought entered my head. The thought was strong enough to cause me to stop. I sensed it was profound, yet its literal form—the actual words that popped into my head—seemed almost simplistic.

The words were, *Oh well, there's always God.*

Compared to Saul falling from his horse on the road to Damascus and hearing the Lord bellow, "Saul, Saul, why do you persecute me?" the words I heard appear meager, even tentative.

Oh well, there's always God.

Unlike in Saul's situation, the words were not apparently spoken in the voice of God. I don't know whose voice spoke them. Maybe it was my own voice that had been suppressed for so long. Maybe it was the voice of my subconscious. The words had a tantalizing tone. Because they weren't harsh, judgmental, or absolute, they had powerful appeal. I heard them more as a whisper than a command. They sounded like the concluding line of a poem or the answer to a riddle. They contained an innocence, a sweetness, a softness of expression that made the phrase linger long in my thoughts.

These were easy words, reassuring words, words of optimism and hope. Words that welcomed me back to a language I had lost. Words that welcomed me home. Words that warmed a heart grown cold.

Oh well, there's always God.

So strong were the words, so deep their impact on me, I had to sit down on the staircase and reflect for a while. What did the words exactly mean?

I had gone away but God hadn't. God can't go away. God simply is. His presence is eternal. He is the great I Am. I thought of the story of the prodigal son in which the father welcomes his child with open arms. It matters not that the son had gone astray. The father's love never wanes. The father's acceptance is absolute.

Similarly, I had been taught as a child that God's love and acceptance are not conditional. We don't win his favor with our loyal support or exemplary behavior. His grace is our gift. Grace is an operation of life as simple as the air we breathe. It can't be seen, but with it comes life that words can't describe. It isn't a question of earning or deserving it. Like his presence, it simply is. Our choice is whether to turn from that grace or embrace it fully.

I had turned from the full spectrum of God's gracious ways. In that turning, I had been mired in a difficult marriage with Duane, one during which I had no faith to call upon. I had left that marriage for good reasons. My life had become static and I ceased to feel joy. Joy returned in the person of Waylon Jennings. I was crazy for this man in every respect. Our romance was real and our marriage, no matter how challenging, was something to which I felt permanently committed.

But that romance was not without great challenges. Waylon was like Texas. He was a country unto himself. Most of the time he was emotionally available to me, but not always. One of the things he liked to say to me, referring to the complexity of his mind-set, was "You should see how it looks from in here." I respected that complexity. When it came to Waylon, I required more patience, more understanding, more compassion. If I were to remain in this marriage—as I deeply desired—I needed help.

Sitting on that staircase, I had to wonder: *Could God be the very help I need? Could it be that simple?* The questions themselves relaxed me. They came as a relief. I sighed. I smiled. I even chuckled.

My heart knew that going back to God required no readmission test. I would not have to stand before a committee and answer questions about my truancy. I would face no inquisition or examination. But what would I have to do?

"The truth," I remember my mother saying over and over again, "is in his Word. His Word enlightens even as it heals."

Enlightening and healing were what I sought. *Oh well, there's always God* was a good thought. Now I needed a good word. It was clear that I needed to open the Good Book that I had shelved years earlier.

But on that day, alone in the basement of our house, I didn't run upstairs and break out the Bible. I didn't jump in the car and roar off to church. I didn't call my mother and tell her that I was suddenly back in the fold. I just kept this quiet revelation to myself.

Making my way through the rest of the day, I silently repeated the phrase.

One modest thought.

One plain idea.

One path forward.

One startling insight.

Five heartfelt words.

Oh well, there's always God.

Chapter 15

STORMS NEVER LAST

THE STORY OF MY RELATIONSHIP WITH WAYLON IS ALL IN MY songs. In the first half of the seventies, a dynamically creative period for us both, I wrote more prolifically than at any time before or since. I wrote because I had to. Writing was the only way to voice the warring factions in my mind. Writing was my way of crying and coping, of celebrating and mourning, of hoping and healing. Writing kept me from reacting with impulsive rage or vindictive anger. Writing kept me from morbidity or depression. Writing kept me sane.

Because I was reconsidering my faith, I was already in an introspective space. Taken as a whole, the songs I birthed bear all my contradictory attitudes. I wrote enough original songs to fill two whole albums, thus eschewing the need for covers. Both those albums—*I'm Jessi Colter* and *Jessi*—were recorded for Capitol and coproduced by Waylon and Ken Mansfield, a leading producer who'd worked with the Beach Boys and the Beatles, not to mention Merle Haggard and Buck Owens.

Some wondered why Waylon himself didn't produce me. The reason was wisdom. When it came to my music, he knew that he lacked objectivity. He thought everything I did was great, even those songs that expressed my equivocation about him. He figured that a more dispassionate and experienced producer would serve me better.

Ken was great. Like Chet Atkins, he was extremely supportive of my artistry. He saw my deep involvement in writing and saw no reason to include outside songs.

"Your record needs to make a personal statement," he said. "And since your songs couldn't be more personal, let's include them all."

That statement was music to my ears—the music I had made and was going to make in my own peculiar mode of self-therapy.

I suppose the most therapeutic of this early batch of songs was one I wrote based on a caption from a magazine I'd seen in a doctor's office. After a tornado had devastated her home, in a moment of brave hope, a resident said, "Storms never last."

Well, due to rumors regarding Waylon, my marriage had already suffered several tornadoes. Yet he was always happy to have me on the road with him where he featured me as part of the show.

I made most of those trips, but not all. There were times when my responsibility for Jennifer and for Waylon's children required that I stay home. When Waylon was home, he was always respectful of me. But when on those very few occasions he was out on the road without me, the rumors would start again—he was with still another willing woman. Those stories led to a series of ongoing storms.

When Waylon first heard the song, he rightly predicted it would be a standard. But he didn't like the first line—"Storms never last, do they, Waylon?"

"Change 'Waylon' to 'baby' so it won't be personal."

I followed his advice and, as a result, the song has been sung by many other artists. But nonetheless it was written with Waylon in mind. It is our duet version, sung some years after my initial solo effort, that I cherish above all others:

Storms never last do they, baby
Bad times all pass with the winds
Your hand in mine steals the thunder
You make the sun want to shine

I followed you down so many roads, baby
I picked wild flowers and sung you soft sad songs
And every road we took, God knows,
    our search was for the truth
And the storm brewin' now won't be the last

The last line—"the storm brewin' now won't be the last"—proved prophetic.

As I listen to many of the songs that emerged from the early years of my marriage to Waylon, I distinctly remember first feeling one way, and then another. In songs like "You Ain't Never Been Loved (Like I'm Going to Love You)," I expressed steely determination that the strength of my love was great enough for the both of us. Yet in "Is There Any Way You'll Stay Forever?"—a soul rocker—uncertainty crops up:

You're a man who does his walkin' like
    he's got some place to go
You're a man who does his talkin' like he
    knows something I don't know
You're a man whose hand I'd hold down any lonely road
Is there any way you'll stay forever?

Some of these songs can be understood literally. I really did believe that Waylon had never been loved by anyone as I loved him; I really did worry whether he would stay forever. Yet other songs employed stories with other proper names. I employed these other names not to mask my feelings, but to create more dramatic settings. Underneath the mask, the writer's emotions were on full display.

The most complex and at the same time simplest of these songs turned out later to be among my best known. It was a slow, mournful ballad and didn't become a hit until years after I wrote it. Its theme concerned confused identity. I called it "I'm Not Lisa."

> I'm not Lisa, my name is Julie
> Lisa left you years ago
> My eyes are not blue, but mine won't leave you
> Till the sunlight has touched your face
>
> She was your morning light
> Her smile told of no night
> Your love for her grew
> With each rising sun
>
> And then one winter day, his hand led her away
> She left you here drowning in your tears
> Here, where you've stayed for years
> Crying, Lisa, Lisa

Of course I'm not Lisa or Julie. In fact, I'm not really Jessi. I'm Mirriam. But Jessi the writer imagined Julie the lover whose man confused her for another. I could picture Waylon easily confusing me for someone else in his past. I didn't accuse him of doing so—and I wasn't even convinced that he had. But I could imagine it. I could imagine it enough to weave the story into a song.

I could also imagine a woman searching for a man who had left her but now seeks to find her. Waylon had deep brown eyes, so in this song—to make certain it would not be taken literally—I took poetic license in depicting lost love. I asked, "What's Happened to Blue Eyes?"

I'm looking for blue eyes, has anyone seen him?
Don't you tell me, he gave up on me
I'm looking for blue eyes, I've got to find him
Oh something tells me, he's looking for me

There was a time when blue eyes
    said there was no other
His one and only love he swore I'd be
There was a time when his blue eyes
    saw clearer than mine did
Storms and rain, tears and pain, bring me back his way

Love lost and found, passing storms, uncertain identity, certain commitments, broken promises, unbroken devotion—these were the subjects that preoccupied me as I settled into my unsettling roles as writer, wife, mother, lover, recording artist, and costar.

Chapter 16

OUTLAW

My own career, as exciting as it was in the early seventies, never took precedent over my primary concern, my family.

My mother, then sixty-nine, was not in the best physical health, while her spiritual health was more robust than ever. Waylon would often fly her and Dad to Nashville for long visits. Many were the times Waylon and I came crawling in from an all-night songwriting session in the studio, only to be greeted by my mother, fresh as a daisy. When she looked at me with those loving eyes of hers, I never felt ridicule or judgment. I saw Jesus.

I cherish the memory of coming upon Mother, who, spotting a pair of Waylon's boots in the hall closet, took them out, lay hands over them, and blessed them.

"These boots represent the man's strength," she said. "Now I ask God to watch over him and let him know the true source of strength."

My parents also enjoyed coming to our shows and had nothing but praise for our music.

After one particular show, Mother came into my dressing room.

"I know that God is doing a work in you," she said.

"How can you tell?" I asked.

"I had a dream and God showed me you saying, 'It's so hard coming home.' I can feel your spirit lightening, sweetheart. You've been carrying some heavy baggage. I can only imagine the freedom that comes when you put down the bags and walk in the light."

"I can't explain why I ever moved away from that light."

"You don't have to explain. People move in and out of shadows. Some get stuck in the darkness. But you're not the kind to get stuck, Mirriam. You're always on the go. You've been that way ever since you were a little girl. You're a searcher. And you know what you're searching for."

"I do?"

"Of course you do, dear. You're searching for yourself in God. God surrounds us. He's everywhere. He doesn't get lost. We do."

When I mentioned to Mother that I had attended church in Nashville, it didn't at all bother her that, unlike her nondenominational pentecostal services, this congregation was Baptist.

"I bet they sing some of the same hymns you sang growing up," said Mother.

"Yes, and I love them!"

"It's music that brought you to God, Mirriam, and it's music that will bring you back."

Waylon's music was evolving in ways I found thrilling. But the thrills had come at a cost. In 1972, he contracted hepatitis from a dental treatment gone awry. For months he walked around in pain. After so many years of exhausting travel, he was spent.

"Sometimes I feel like it's over," he told me. "How many years can I keep bangin' around the honky-tonks? The IRS is on my tail, not to mention my ex-wives. Far as record sales, I never get ahead of the studio costs and packaging fees they pile on. Besides, I think I've gone about as far as I can go with Chet."

I'm certain that Chet Atkins loved Waylon. The two men had great respect for each other. But Chet had had a hard time with artists

OUTLAW

who, like Waylon, he labeled as pill-heads. The designation wasn't in-accurate. Brilliant singer-songwriters like Don Gibson and Roger Miller, the funniest man in Nashville, had given Chet fits. Their volatility ran counter to Chet's laid-back disposition. Chet trafficked in calmness while these guys were nothing if not hyper.

After several years of working with Waylon, Chet grew weary. He wanted to put Waylon on a schedule while making sure Waylon's sound conformed with Chet's highly successful Nashville sound. That often meant imposing sweet strings—often *sugary* sweet strings—and back-ground singers for soothing harmonies.

But Waylon wasn't interested in anything sugary or smooth. He often said that in those days Nashville's kind of assembly-line music was trying too hard to be pretty, while he was determined to stay raw. Waylon wanted to rock. Waylon wanted to lay bare his troubled soul in songs that did not necessarily fit in with Chet's time-honored system. Waylon also didn't want to be restricted to recording in Chet's corporate studio. He found that environment stifling. Finally, and most critically, Waylon wanted to challenge Nashville's locked-in business procedures. He thought his con-tract was weighted on the side of the record company. He wanted creative freedom and a bigger piece of the financial pie.

As long as Lucky Moeller was running Waylon's career, nothing much changed. Lucky was a get-along, go-along fixture in the coun-try music establishment. It was enough if his artists kept touring and recording. He had no interest in rewriting the playbook.

Neil Reshen, an accountant-manager from New York City, relished rewriting the playbook. Waylon's drummer Richie Albright had made the introduction, telling Waylon, "You're not going to like or trust this guy, but hire him. It'll be the best thing you ever did."

When Waylon and I met Neil, we understood what Richie meant. He was a fast-talking New Yorker with a distinctly un-Nashville demea-nor. Nothing laid-back about him. From the first remark on, Neil was in your face.

"I need to be in RCA's face," he said. "I need to be in Chet Aktins's face. I need to hit RCA with an audit."

The audit was Neil's specialty. He explained how in working with clients as different as Miles Davis, Frank Zappa, and the Mothers of Invention, he had assaulted record companies head-on.

"They're snakes," he said. "They cheat, they connive, they hide money, they generate rigged royalty statements. Their chief goal is to charge every possible expense against you so you wind up with minus earnings."

"Hoss," Waylon told Neil, "you're preaching to the choir."

Then Waylon turned to me and asked, "What do you think, hon?"

"I think Mr. Neil Reshen is just the man we need."

Our instincts proved right. Neil's energy boosted Waylon out of the doldrums. Unlike Lucky Moeller, Neil couldn't care less about alienating the powers-that-be. His forceful negotiations turned the Nashville establishment on its ear. Within a remarkably short period of time, he'd renegotiated Waylon's royalty rate, improving it dramatically. He also won his demands that Waylon be given creative freedom and the right to record wherever he wanted. In short, it was an across-the-board victory.

Lonesome, On'ry and Mean was the first in a series of brilliant Waylon records to come. He sang scorching versions of Johnny Cash's "Gone to Denver," Willie Nelson's "Pretend I Never Happened," and Kris Kristofferson's "Me and Bobby McGee." The most startling thing about the album, though, might have been the cover. The clean-cut Waylon was gone. The new Waylon had long hair and a scruffy beard.

"Hope you don't mind the new look, darlin'," he said to me.

I couldn't have cared less. "You couldn't be bad-looking if you tried," I said.

When Mother saw the new image, though, she was less forgiving.

"Son," she said, "that beard and mustache sure looks like a bunch of nasty ants going to a funeral."

It was a little shocking to hear Mother talk that way. On the other hand, for all her spiritual devotion, she had no problem telling it like it is.

Neil Reshen did more than rewrite Waylon's record deal. He also booked him in places he'd never played before—like Max's Kansas City in Manhattan, the home of cutting-edge rock like the New York Dolls and Velvet Underground. Waylon looked out into the audience and saw a gender-bender crowd of freakish proportions. He almost freaked himself.

"What are they gonna think of me?" he asked.

"They're gonna love you," I answered.

And sure enough, the downtown avant-garde hipsters loved Waylon and laughed when he told them, "Hope you like my music, but if you don't, don't say nothing mean 'cause if you do and ever show up in Nashville, we'll kick your backside."

From that point on, there was virtually no venue Waylon couldn't play and no audience he couldn't win over.

We worked the Troubadour in Hollywood, ground zero for the LA singer-songwriter crowd, and opened for the Grateful Dead on a national tour. The deadheads loved Waylon, and so did the Hell's Angels, who began showing up in droves. Two Hell's Angels—Boomer Baker and Deakon Proudfoot—became the backbone of our devoted security team. When Waylon sang his sad songs, the Angels weren't ashamed to cry openly.

In addition to upgrading Waylon's bookings, Neil also garnered him national press in *Time* and *Newsweek*. Somewhere along the line, Hazel Smith, a local publicist who championed Waylon's music, christened his art as Outlaw. The name stuck. It seemed to apply not only to Waylon but to other artists working outside the tight-and-narrow Nashville box—Willie Nelson, Kris Kristofferson, and Tompall Glaser.

Waylon wasn't entirely comfortable with the designation because of his inherent dislike of all labels. At the same time, when he saw it catching on, he understood its value.

"After all," he said, "when Bob Dylan wrote in 'John Wesley Harding' that 'to live outside the law you must be honest,' I could certainly relate."

When it came to Outlaw Country, Waylon never claimed to be its first practitioner. He credited Hank Williams. He always spoke lovingly of Hank's Luke the Drifter recitations, "Pictures from Life's Other Side" and "Too Many Parties and Too Many Pals."

"Anything I do in Nashville," Waylon would say in practically every interview, "is nothing compared to Hank. We're all living in his long, lanky shadow."

Waylon's most abiding Outlaw buddy was Willie Nelson. Leaving Nashville for Austin, Willie had tapped into a younger alternative audience without alienating more traditional fans. Willie and Waylon had more in common than their Texas birthrights. They were both rebels, both rugged individualists, both tied to the deepest roots of American music without conforming to any one style. They both thought they could sing anything. And they could.

Also like Waylon, Willie never fit into the Nashville mode. It wasn't until he left Chet Atkins and RCA and started making records like *Shotgun Willie*, *Phases and Stages*, and *Red Headed Stranger* that he came into his own as a solo artist. These were albums that both influenced and were influenced by the classic Waylon records that were released in the same early seventies time frame: *Honky Tonk Heroes*, *This Time*, *The Ramblin' Man*, and *Dreaming My Dreams*.

Willie's first Fourth of July Picnic in Dripping Springs, Texas, in 1973 was a watershed event, bringing together hillbillies, hippies, rednecks, radicals, and everyone in between. Waylon and I were on the bill.

Waylon's friendship with Willie, like his friendship with Johnny Cash, was deep. They had only an occasional disagreement. I used to say, "Willie and Waylon have a stupid love." No doubt, Waylon had a soft spot for Willie. At the same time, there was a slight undercurrent of competition, but their musical souls were aligned. When it came to taking on the music business, they were comrades in arms. I saw them as daring and brave artists who forged the future of country music, even as they honored its past.

<hr />

At the same time this Outlaw movement was gaining speed, I was looking to anchor our family in more comfortable quarters. In 1973, we moved to a five-bedroom home built in the twenties on Stokes Lane in the heart of the Green Hills section of Nashville. It was close to the Glaser Sound Studio where Waylon was doing much of his recording with Tompall Glaser and just around the corner from the studio of Jack "Cowboy" Clement.

Tompall was Waylon's primary pinball opponent and a supreme smart aleck. I got to watch some of those pinball marathons, held at Burger Boy or J.J.'s Market on Broadway or lonesome truck stops out Route 65. They were hilarious. The barbs never stopped. Neither did the playing, except for a breakfast break at two or three in the morning. When the boys got too cross-eyed and groggy to play another game, they'd retire to Tompall's office where they'd meet up with Bobby Bare or Captain Midnight, the famed Nashville deejay and country music scholar, or Texas renegade Kinky Friedman. It was always a blast.

Cowboy Clement not only became part of Waylon's inner circle and one of his go-to producers, he became my brother-in-law! My sister Sharon met Cowboy while visiting us in Nashville. Her magnetic personality had never failed to attract beguiling men, and Cowboy was beyond charismatic. He was also one of the great producers of American music. Waylon described him as "part of the incredible vortex of energy that was Sun Records, a man who'd produced everyone from Jerry Lee Lewis to Johnny Cash to Charlie Pride."

"He's crazier than a loon," Waylon told me, "but I'm sure you're going to love him."

I did. But Sharon loved him even more. Their whirlwind romance soon got serious. In their frenzied imaginations, they saw each other in a dazzling light: Sharon thought Cowboy was a movie producer and Cowboy thought Sharon was a movie star. In fact, they were stars in their own madcap movie. They married just months after they met and divorced not too many months after that. While they were together, the fireworks never stopped.

By the time we moved from Stokes Lane to a secluded modern house just off Granny White Pike, high in Forest Hills with beautiful views overlooking Nashville, Sharon and Cowboy were history. History was much on my mind during this time because the real Granny White was a widow named Lucinda White who ran a tavern, once located close to our home, where in the late eighteenth century she had often hosted Andrew Jackson. Driving down the road, I often thought about Lucinda and the fabulous frontier characters who must have frequented her establishment.

I wanted to stay close to home, but the road always called. To live with Waylon, to be with Waylon, to love Waylon with the kind of love he required meant being on the road. And while I had some resistance, I also couldn't deny the pleasure that the road afforded. There was a flow to life on the road that, once I surrendered to its rhythms, provided a certain comfort. Most comforting of all was the knowledge that—despite the unexpected detours and speed bumps—Waylon and I were rolling down the road together.

At the same time, I don't want to overlook those detours and speed bumps. They could be both dangerous and maddening. How did I cope with them? The answer, as I've noted, is in my songs.

Chapter 17

OF MAN AND GOD

I WAS WORKING ON TWO CRITICAL ENDEAVORS AT THE SAME time: my marriage to Waylon and my renewed relationship with God. Both endeavors were complicated, both involved internal conflicts, and both deeply influenced the music I was making.

In the midseventies, I was writing two albums at once. They each carried my name, although those names were different. One album was called *Jessi*, the other *Mirriam*.

Jessi was the wife of Waylon and the artist who had recorded two secular albums. Mirriam was the follower of Christ returning to her faith. Because I was both Jessi and Mirriam, I could not give up one for the other. All I could do was allow each to have her say.

Jessi was my third album and the second for Capitol. Ken Mansfield produced it with help from Waylon. I wrote the music and lyrics for all ten songs. The first composition set the tone. I called it "The Hand That Rocks the Cradle."

> In the wee small hours of midnight
> When your man just won't come home

With your legs spread on his bed
Howlin' at the moon
When the hot blood in your body
Is tryin' to flood your mind
Let the hand that rocks the cradle lead your song

On first blush, it seems to be a story about a woman trying to come to terms with a wayward man, a woman looking to be led by a primal force that may not be that man at all. That force may be God. Isn't God the hand that rocks the cradle? Isn't the left-home-alone woman seeking a spiritual salvation?

And yet in "Here I Am," the woman is offering nothing more than a simple love song to her man:

You walk away into the sunset
You stop, take one last look at me
I feel that look wash warm all over
Here I am, here I'll stay

We've been together but a short time
Your fingertips have learned my face
Your hands on me have lightened every darkened place
Here I am, here I'll stay

This is the same woman who, overwhelmed with anxiety after having passed the night alone, finds herself still being able to say, "It's morning and I still love you."

Like a dream I thought
The sun would find you gone
It's morning and I still love you

Yet the impassioned commitment I wrote about in these and other songs like "All My Life, I've Been Your Lady" and "One-Woman Man" are set against stories like "Rounder" that openly expressed my anxiety.

> You know he must get tired of tasting dust
> You know how long he's stalked the night
> trying hard to trust
> You know you ain't made a man to carry that load
> You know how tired he must be getting
> of hiding in the road
>
> Oh my Lord, don't leave that Rounder alone
> And my Lord, need you to bring him all the way home

Even in *Jessi*, my secular album, I was sending up prayers. I'm saying that I've not only been loving Waylon, but I've been loving God. Those prayers helped mitigate my fear of losing Waylon, who, despite his antics, I knew to be my one and only soul mate.

In picturing life without him, I wrote:

> Without you I can't go on
> Without you I've got no song to sing
> Without you standing there
> I don't even care for anything
> Without all the love you give
> You won't find me wantin' much to live

On the sacred side, my heart cried for God. Sitting alone at the piano when I was able to steal a few hours of solitude, I found myself meditating on the love I had felt for the Lord as a child and wondering where that love had gone. Tears filled my eyes as I wrote:

God, if I could only write your love song
I would leave it here on earth so you could hear
I know you hear my words, you hear my music too
Could it be you'd like to hear me loving you?

I had been attending church on a more regular basis, sometimes going to the Church of Christ on Sixteenth Avenue where Don Finto was the minister. I saw Don more as a missionary than a minister. Many churches say, "All are welcome," but not all churches mean it. Don meant it. There was no dress code. The more casual, the better. The pews were filled with folks from every walk of life. There were hippies and artists, the infirm and the addicted, the affluent and the homeless. Don embraced anyone seeking the comfort of God. He led what some began calling the Jesus Movement that heralded the inclusiveness and all-loving essence of God. Don preached against pharisaical doctrines that elevated legalism over love.

Inspired by both the message and warmth of Don's beautiful ministry, I wrote "Let It Go" in an upbeat, celebratory mood.

There ain't no shame you are carrying
    can make him stop loving you
And there ain't no wrong you've done
    he won't forgive you
He knows our body's made of dust,
    he knows our days are few

Let it go, turn it loose

I sought solace in Presbyterian churches where I discovered a new joy in reading litanies. I'd go to Catholic churches where the solemn beauty of Mass stirred my soul. I'd also have fellowship with Messianic Jewish believers whose passion for Christ had its own kind of power.

I loved seeing how they married the Old Testament to the New. The more I was witness to different ways of worshipping, the more I felt myself drawn to the one true God.

In that spirit, I wrote "Put Your Arms Around Me."

> Put your arms around me
> Let me know you know me
> Let me hear you call me by my name
>
> I'm so ashamed I ever doubted
> That you and me and me and you and
>   love would find the way
> There was a time I swore life was one big heartache
>
> There was a time I said good had up and gone
> There was a time I said there is no God in heaven
> Till every prayer I prayed came bringing me the sun

I sang "I'm so ashamed I ever doubted," and shame was certainly part of the emotional baggage that I carried in my return to faith. When I attended the Greater Apostolic Christ Church, though, my shame quickly dissipated. That's because Apostolic was a full-gospel congregation of African American Christians whose praise and worship was absolutely overwhelming. Being the only white worshipper made no difference.

I'd learned about the church from an African American woman, our housekeeper Jane. She was a prayer warrior and steely strong believer. In fact, when Jane heard Waylon complain about my going to church, she said, "Honey, my husband used to beat me for going to church. But that didn't change my mind. You just have to be sweet and live it."

Greater Apostolic became my main Christian home for two decades. It was where I lived it. Every Sunday I couldn't wait for services to start.

Reverend Harris would lay it on the line, an impassioned preacher who, much like my mom, had the gifts of the Spirit. Passion washed over every inch of that sanctuary. The teaching was vivid and direct. And the music, the ever-positive, ever-joyful, ever-inspiring gospel music lifted me out of my seat and had me singing and praising God along with the rest of the congregation. Oh, how I loved it when we sang "Can't No One Do You Like Jesus"!

I wasn't made to feel self-conscious or treated as an outsider. I was accepted as family. When I wrote and recorded "There Ain't No Rain in God," I had the full support of the soaring Greater Apostolic mass choir behind me. What a thrill!

> There ain't no rain in God
> He made the sunshine just for you
> Don't let those storm clouds brew
> Don't let this world get to you
>
> When darkness creeps all around
> Hate his face and put him down
> Don't you know you're on God's ground
> And there ain't no rain in God

It was at Greater Apostolic that I renewed my childhood faith in the holy ritual of praise and worship. You came to praise his goodness and worship his love. When the praising and worshipping was over, you left that church feeling more alive—a hundred times more alive—than when you entered.

The moment of full return, the moment when the deepest part of my heart knew that I had recovered my lost faith, happened in a flash. It was late at night and I was seated at the piano. I wasn't sure what notes to play or what words to write. I simply felt that I was close to some breakthrough. So I closed my eyes and offered up a prayer. I didn't ask

Helen D. Perkins at 16,
a coal miner's daughter
with a heart for God.

FROM AUTHOR'S
PERSONAL COLLECTION.

Arnold Johnson, at 18,
inventor and dreamer.

FROM AUTHOR'S
PERSONAL COLLECTION.

My father in Indiana, victorious in a car that he built himself.

FROM AUTHOR'S PERSONAL COLLECTION.

Here I am at age 3, a blessed child in Mesa, Arizona.

FROM AUTHOR'S PERSONAL COLLECTION.

Our home, a former army barracks, was also our church.

FROM AUTHOR'S PERSONAL COLLECTION.

My beautiful big sister Sharon, at age 10, standing next to me, at age 8. She's got the best doll.

FROM AUTHOR'S PERSONAL COLLECTION.

Preaching the gospel, Mother was an anointed servant of God.

FROM AUTHOR'S PERSONAL COLLECTION.

My father's mine, all twelve hundred acres, was a deep part of my childhood. It was Daddy's lifelong quest and passion.

FROM AUTHOR'S PERSONAL COLLECTION.

My first promotional
picture. Mirriam
Johnson at 17.

COURTESY OF
BRUNO OF HOLLYWOOD.

I married Duane Eddy at the Tropicana in Las Vegas. From the left,
sisters Helen and Sharon, musician Jim Horn, the bride, the groom,
best friend Sonja Hanson, and best man Dick Clark.

FROM AUTHOR'S PERSONAL COLLECTION.

My darling daughter Jennifer. I learned that a little child could guide and anchor me in love.

FROM AUTHOR'S PERSONAL COLLECTION.

He was my cowboy. Clean-shaven Waylon at the start of our lifelong love affair.

PHOTO COURTESY OF HOPE POWELL.

Chet Atkins called my first album *A Country Star Is Born.* I loved Chet but found the title a bit much.

PHOTO COURTESY OF JIMMY MOORE.

A precious moment in time: The Frontier was the best sound room in Vegas. On the show we were lucky to have Roger Miller, the funniest man in country.

FROM AUTHOR'S PERSONAL COLLECTION.

Recording *I'm Jessi Colter.* Singing my very own songs was an extravagant pleasure.

USED BY PERMISSION. GETTY IMAGES. MICHAEL OCHS ARCHIVES.

It was the midseventies and I was riding high. At a banquet honoring "I'm Not Lisa" with BMI exec Frances Preston. Standing next to Waylon is his manager Neil Reshen.

PHOTO COURTESY OF BROADCAST MUSIC ARCHIVE.

Waylon and Willie set Austin on fire and forged a very special relationship.

PHOTO COURTESY OF MELINDA WICKMAN.

Waylon Albright Jennings, born of our love on May 19, 1979. We called him Shooter.

PHOTO CREDIT: NASHVILLE PUBLIC LIBRARY, SPECIAL COLLECTIONS.

Mohammed Ali attended Shooter's christening. Waylon, who idolized the Greatest, couldn't have been more thrilled.

PHOTOGRAPH BY JAMES MINCHIN III.

I was delighted to throw a fifties-themed sobriety party for Johnny Cash. Kris Kristofferson is on guitar with Rodney Crowell, Rosanne Cash, and Johnny and June looking on.

PHOTO COURTESY OF BILLY MITCHELL (WWW.BILLYMITCHELL.COM).

That same sobriety party at Southern Comfort—Kris, Johnny, wide-eyed Willie, Hank Williams Jr., and my man in his fifties formal attire.

PHOTO COURTESY OF BILLY MITCHELL (WWW.BILLYMITCHELL.COM).

Two lovebirds
at play.

PHOTO COURTESY OF
MELINDA WICKMAN.

After Waylon got sober, he bought himself a gold Cadillac, quipping,
"From one nose to another."

FROM AUTHOR'S PERSONAL COLLECTION.

In Tucson, during the filming of *Stagecoach*, we put on western gear and had a ball. You'll recognize Waylon, John Schneider from *Dukes of Hazzard*, Johnny Cash, John Carter, Anthony Newley, and our goddaughter Haley Hyatt. I'm next to Mary Crosby while Shooter plays cards on the floor.

FROM AUTHOR'S PERSONAL COLLECTION.

The master at work.

PHOTO COURTESY OF MELINDA WICKMAN.

If country music had a Mt. Rushmore, it would look like this: Highwaymen Waylon, Johnny, Willie, and Kris.

PHOTO BY JIM MCGUIRE. COURTESY OF SONY MUSIC ENTERTAINMENT.

Waylon always wanted a "decent wedding" and surprised me with this ceremony on our 25th anniversary. From left, Kathy and Buddy Jennings, Deana and Josie Jennings, Deborah, Terry and Josh Jennings, the bride and groom, Shooter, Julie and Taylor Jennings, my daughter Jennifer and son Will, and Tomi Lynne Jennings.

PHOTO COURTESY OF BILLY MITCHELL (WWW.BILLYMITCHELL.COM).

My husband liked nothing more than hanging out at Southern Comfort and writing his heart out.

FROM AUTHOR'S PERSONAL COLLECTION.

After Waylon made his crossing, my immediate family gathered around me and kept me whole.

FROM AUTHOR'S PERSONAL COLLECTION.

Waylon's good buddy Hank Williams Jr. came to Scottsdale where the two of us paid tribute to Waylon.

PHOTO COURTESY OF BILLY MITCHELL (WWW.BILLYMITCHELL.COM).

What a joy to compose with my son, Shooter! Here we are writing a song for *The Passion of the Christ*, "Please Carry Me Home."

FROM AUTHOR'S PERSONAL COLLECTION.

Walking the landscape of my beloved Arizona during a photo shoot for *Out of the Ashes*, my album produced by the wonderful Don Was.

PHOTOGRAPH BY JAMES MINCHIN III.

Whenever I needed him, he came running. Kris is more than a great artist; he's a true friend.

FROM AUTHOR'S PERSONAL COLLECTION.

Backstage at the fabulous "All for the Hall" show. From left, Trace Adkins, Tim McGraw, Kris Kristofferson, Keith Urban, Vince Gill, me, Billy Joe Shaver, Rosanne Cash, Eric Church, Troy Gentry, Eddie Montgomery, and Hank Williams Jr.

FROM AUTHOR'S PERSONAL COLLECTION.

A girl's best friend. Cowgirl comes from a long line of champion red fox Labradors. She's my baby.

PHOTO COURTESY OF CHARLES GABREAN.

for inspiration. In fact, I didn't ask for anything specific. I just prayed the way Jesus had taught me to pray. Praying for God's will, I wrote:

> God, I love you
> God, I need you
> Would you find a way to stay close today?
>
> If I walk a little softer, if I try much harder
> To see your face in everything today
> Will you stay a little closer
> So I can hear you if you whisper?
> Would you find a way to stay right close today?

The songs I wrote for *Mirriam* washed over me with an energy I had never felt before. They came quickly and powerfully. Because they were so emotionally draining, they left me almost numb. It wasn't that I didn't love writing them—I have never loved songwriting so much before or since—yet I felt more like a vessel than a writer.

All the songs but one focused on my relationship with God. And the gift God afforded me was the opportunity to sing that one exceptional song to the person for whom it was written: Mother.

Because we spent so much time on the road, we rented rather than bought our houses in Nashville. I lost count of how many times we moved. It was to our Saxon Drive home that Mother came in 1974 for a visit. I had just completed recording demos of all the songs for *Mirriam*.

One evening after dinner I asked her into the living room.

"There's some music I'd like you to hear," I said.

"A new record of yours?" she asked.

"Yes."

At the time, my first album for Capitol—*I'm Jessi Colter*—had been released, and my second album—*Jessi*—was completed. Mother had heard and praised this music. There was never a hint of disapproval.

She'd never urged me to record religious songs. Nor had I told her that for many months now I had been doing just that.

As she sat on the living room couch and the music poured from the speakers, she smiled radiantly and nodded her head to the rhythms, her eyes moist.

"Praise God," she said. "Praise God who has answered my prayers more abundantly than I could have ever imagined."

"There's one song," I said, "that you haven't heard. That's a song I'd like to play for you right now. Would you come sit next to me at the piano?"

"Of course, sweetheart. When I see you at the piano, I see my little girl playing in our church. My little girl who had been blessed by God with a gift to sing his praises."

"This song doesn't sing God's praise," I explained. "This song is for you."

With Mother seated next to me on the piano bench, I ran my fingers over the keys and sang:

> My mama is a mama you'd believe in
> As a child I remember how she prayed
> Often misunderstood she lived lonely
> But my mama believes God's holy Word
>
> Mama knows no strangers, she knows Jesus
> And everyone's God's children in her eyes
> A bluebird's broken wing or a man that's hurt and dying
> My mama trusts God for everything

When I finished singing, neither of us spoke. We simply sat there, Mother's hand on mine.

Chapter 18

JOY AND GRIEF

IN 1975, MY MUSICAL CAREER SKYROCKETED IN A MANNER I never could have anticipated. Everything happened at once.

A single from the *I'm Jessi Colter* album suddenly took off and reached number three on the pop chart. I was surprised, not because I didn't like "I'm Not Lisa"—I always loved the song—but because I considered its confused identity theme a bit offbeat. No matter, along with the Captain and Tennille's "Love Will Keep Us Together," Glen Campbell's "Rhinestone Cowboy," David Bowie's "Fame," and Earth, Wind and Fire's "Shining Star," it became one of the biggest hits of the year.

Waylon couldn't have been happier.

"Baby," he said, "you got yourself a pop smash that makes you a bigger star than me. Man, I couldn't go pop with a mouthful of firecrackers."

I had no desire to be more popular than Waylon and, in fact, I was not. His fan base was broad, deep, and devoted. "I'm Not Lisa" certainly brought me more name recognition, but it did not reshape my ambition. I was happy to be featured during Waylon's show.

During one such show at the Santa Monica Civic Auditorium, I had a phenomenal experience. This came at a point when "I'm Not

Lisa" was at its height. Waylon designated a section of the show to highlight the song. A black Steinway grand, covered with dozens of long-stemmed white roses, was rolled out. That night I wore an exquisite shawl dress with elaborate fringe trim. I was excited—almost too excited—and also apprehensive.

Maybe it was the pressure that comes with a hit song. Maybe it was the lead position that I was suddenly assuming. Maybe it was the fact that Waylon was highlighting me so dramatically. Whatever the reasons, it was unusual for me to feel a sudden sense of insecurity. My mind was a mess. Would a live performance be as good as the record itself? Would the audience be disappointed? Would a subpar rendition prove the hit was a fluke?

A flood of emotions washed over me as I walked to the piano at center stage. A hush fell over the audience. I took a deep breath. And then another. And then a third. And then—to my own surprise—I found myself kneeling in front of the piano. I stayed on my knees for at least a minute. No one quite knew what I was doing. But I did. I was praying. I was praying for strength, for calmness, for resolve, for energy.

God answered my prayer. He visited me. He entered my heart and quieted my mind. He stripped me of the burden of self-concern that had been weighing so heavily on my psyche. He set me free. It was an experience unlike anything I had ever felt. I felt light as air. I felt like a weightless spirit. I felt focused. I felt no fear. I felt an awesome sense of security. I felt as though my heart and God's heart were one. I stood up, went to the piano, and gave the performance of a lifetime. The standing ovation only confirmed what I already knew: I had been transported to another realm.

After God's visitation, I had entered the zone that I sometimes hear athletes describe—where their every move is effortless as they gracefully move toward victory. In this case, the victory was not mine. It was God's.

"Good grief, girl," said Ralph Mooney, the great steel guitarist who'd accompanied me, "looking at you down there on the ground, I was sure you'd fainted."

"Not even close," I said.

"Then what were you doing?" Ralph asked.

"Giving God the glory."

Later I learned that, at the very moment of my performance, my mother, far off on our mine property with Daddy, had sensed my fear and prayed for my comfort. I couldn't imagine life without Mother. Yet in only a few short weeks, that was the harsh reality I found myself facing.

I was home in Nashville when my brother Johnny called to say that Mother had fallen and suffered a cerebral hemorrhage. I flew to Phoenix where she lay in a coma at St. Joseph's, the hospital where I was born. During these last days, it was a blessing to stay by her side. As she made her transition, I saw on her face a beautiful calmness—a radiant glow—that belied all anxiety. I thought of the scripture "Perfect love casts out fear" (1 John 4:18).

Waylon, who loved her dearly, came to her funeral in Mesa, where I sang "When Jesus Comes."

Sister Helen Johnson was eulogized as a woman who strengthened the knees of the lame and opened the eyes of the blind. Deep sadness fused with great joy—sadness that she had left this realm, joy that she was at one with Christ, her bright morning star and the lover of her soul.

In the aftermath of Mother's passing, my worldly successes seemed insignificant. Yet the world went on. I mothered Jennifer, then eleven. I toured. I recorded. My second Capitol album, *Jessi*, was issued on the heels of "I'm Not Lisa" being nominated for two Grammys. Waylon did the lion's share of production work with help from Ken Mansfield.

I had wanted to release *Mirriam* first, but the label thought it risky to change direction so suddenly, especially after I'd hit the pop charts. As *Jessi* entered the Billboard's Top 100, Waylon and I were greeted with still another unexpected surprise: a collection he had put together called *Wanted! The Outlaws* was released, causing an immediate sensation.

It was all Waylon's doing. He'd gone through the vaults and compiled mostly previously recorded tracks by himself, Willie Nelson, Tompall Glaser, and me. Waylon included a duet of us singing "Suspicious Minds" and "I Ain't the One," plus my versions of "I'm Looking for Blue Eyes," "You Mean to Say," "It Ain't Easy," and "Why You Been Gone So Long." Willie's contributions ranged from "Heaven and Hell," the charming "Me and Paul," and the haunting "Healing Hands of Time." Tompall sang "T for Texas" and "Put Another Log on the Fire." Waylon contributed two heroic numbers—"Honky Tonk Heroes (Like Me)" and "My Heroes Have Always Been Cowboys."

Waylon and Willie wrote and sang as a duet the song that ignited it all. "Good Hearted Woman" was a number-one hit and the album became an instant classic, heralded as a hallmark in country music. In its first two weeks, *Wanted! The Outlaws* sold a million copies—the first album in the history of country music to do so—and, before it was over, sales would exceed five million.

The album cover, designed to look like a wanted poster in the post office, had pictures of Waylon, Willie, Tompall, and myself. People asked me what it felt like to be included in a group of so-called ruffians. My answer was always the same—I was honored to be the only gal in the outlaw clan. I was honored because my fellow hooligans were all remarkably talented singer-songwriters.

As far as the handle itself, I didn't take it all that seriously. And neither did Waylon. He understood that while he and Willie had certainly stood firm in the face of Nashville conformity, Music City had taught them a lot. And despite whatever differences they had had with

Nashville production, both Waylon and Willie loved and respected Chet Atkins.

"It's romantic to call someone an outlaw," Waylon once said. "And in this country, romance sells. If you're in the record business and you don't realize the power of promotion, you'd better go back to the farm and start milking cows."

Whether it was the romance of the packaging or the combination of the artists or the selection of the songs, *Wanted! The Outlaws* was a turning point. Country music was never quite the same afterward.

Jessi, my second Capitol album, did so well that they wanted to rush out a third. When I expressed my desire to release *Mirriam*, I heard the same arguments I'd heard before—don't undercut your career by a sudden move in a different direction. I didn't buy the argument. I wasn't looking to protect my career. But the songs I'd recorded for *Mirriam* would always be there. I had every intention of releasing the record. And if that meant waiting another year, so be it.

Given the hurry-up mood surrounding my third Capitol record— *Diamond in the Rough*—I didn't have much time to write. Of the ten songs, only three were new compositions of mine. The rest were covers. I loved the covers, though, especially the deeply soulful title cut by Donnie Fritts and Spooner Oldham. I had fun singing Lennon and McCartney's "Get Back" and "Hey Jude," and especially Lee Emerson's "I Thought I Heard You Calling My Name." Lee was a friend, a great writer with a crazy reputation. Despite—or because of—his idiosyncrasies, we got along well. He once gave me a jukebox crammed with his hits. Tragically, he was shot to death by Barry Sadler, the songwriter of "The Ballad of the Green Berets." They were fighting over a woman.

I continued to fight for my emotional equilibrium, using songs to shore up my spirits. Two of my originals for *Diamond in the Rough* point to the ongoing challenges I faced with Waylon. My love hadn't diminished—it never would—but at times my patience was wearing thin. Waylon's wandering ways hadn't completely stopped. And yet I remained resolute. I stayed. At the same time, I allowed my emotions to wander in songs like "Would You Leave Now."

> I see you leaving
> You see me grieving
> You hear me pleading for you to stay
>
> I see you walking
> Don't you hear me talking
> The tears I'm crying straight from my soul
> Would you leave now before it's over?

I also did not inhibit my humor or my devotion in a song that spoke directly to the man I loved. For the first time in lyrics, I called him by name:

> You did hang the moon, didn't you, Waylon?
>
> Weren't you the one they called the seventh son
> You take so many words and bring
>   them all home with one
> You walk into my room and it lights up like the sun
> Each step you take leads a way for someone
> And I know you'd never do love wrong
>
> You did hang the moon, didn't you, Waylon?

The third original song I wrote for *Diamond in the Rough* was based on fiction rather than fact. I invented a story and imagined a character I called Will. I envisioned him as a man who, through forces greater than himself, rained misery on the woman in his life. It was a plaintive ballad, shot through with pain, "Oh Will (Who Made It Rain Last Night)."

> Oh Will, who made it rain last night
> Who can take the blue from my sky
> And paint it black night?
> Who's telling me to look so I'll see
> The tears for years we will cry
>
> Talk to me, Will, you never told lies
> Who made it rain last night
> His hand in mine, the tears in my eyes
> That won't dry
> And wounds in my heart that won't heal

Will was not Waylon, and yet Waylon, for all his wonderful qualities, was still not the man I wanted him to be.

In the wake of all our great successes—"I'm Not Lisa," the Outlaws record, and Waylon's bestselling *Are You Ready for the Country* album— we were both trying to cope with a heady mix of emotions. We were both dealing with frantically busy schedules. We were both caught up in a blizzard of show business demands.

In the midst of heavy confusion, when it came to Waylon, I had reached the limits of my understanding. We didn't sit down with a counselor. We didn't even discuss it with each other. We just did it.

We separated.

Chapter 19

MIRRIAM

A FRIEND OF MINE IS ALWAYS SAYING, "JUST WHEN YOU THINK you've been patient enough, more patience is required."

I wish I had heard those words in 1976, the year that I was convinced my patience had been exhausted. The cause of the breakup was not Waylon's infidelities or his drug use, although both matters continued to concern me. The cause was my return to faith.

In re-embracing Christ, I felt whole. During my years of wandering, I had sorely missed that blissful feeling. When I reclaimed that feeling, when I could openly and sincerely profess my faith, I did so with firm conviction and boundless enthusiasm. I wanted Waylon to share this faith with me. I wanted him to come back to Jesus, just as I had.

The death of my mother surely contributed to my emotional state. I thanked God that she had been alive to witness my spiritual home-coming. I saw that as one of the great blessings of my adult life. She had been my mother in Christ. Now I longed for Waylon to be my husband in Christ. Without his commitment to God, I didn't see how I could stay with him.

When I approached the subject, he was adamant.

"I like that you've found your way back to the Lord," he said. "It's good to be a believer. And I do believe in something greater than myself. I'd be a fool not to. But I'm not ready to call that something by any name, whether it's Moses, Buddha, Jehovah, or Jesus. I ain't there yet, and maybe will never be."

I came back with arguments. I came back with Scripture. I was well versed in what seemed to me incontrovertible proof of Jesus' divinity. And though I understood how Waylon's early indoctrination into the fire-and-brimstone furnace of fear-based Christianity had repelled him, I soldiered on. I was convinced I could persuade him. When I couldn't, I despaired. I even became angry. In my desire to control Waylon's heart, I overlooked my mother's example of turning control over to God. My intentions were good but my timing was bad. I was headstrong and even self-righteous.

During one phone call when Waylon said something about God I considered untoward, the Spirit rose up in me and I let my husband have it. This was highly unusual. I almost always kept my cool. My verbal expression was so powerful I could practically see Waylon taking ten steps back.

"Wow!" he exclaimed. "I'm gonna watch my tongue. I never want that to happen again."

I'd made my point but I'd also pushed my point too far. It wasn't that Waylon didn't need Jesus. It's my belief that all human souls need Jesus. But was this the right moment and was I the right person to bring him to Jesus? Was I exerting the sensitivity required to accurately read his heart? Or was I, in my insistence, being more self-centered than understanding, more dogmatic about my beliefs than curious about Waylon's?

Although we argued, the arguments didn't last long. There were no verbal fireworks. We both knew that we needed time away from each other. Waylon went his way and I went mine. He slept on the couch in the studio and went on tour without me. I was fine with that. New songs were forming in my head. I visited new churches. I felt neither fear nor remorse. And yet . . .

Waylon Jennings was a man I couldn't stop loving even when I tried. And believe me, I did try. The truth is that I thought about him in the morning when I awoke and in the evening when I went to sleep. I smiled when his music came on the radio. I laughed when I thought about his salty humor. I longed for him. And yet I did not call him. I kept my distance, and he kept his.

The estrangement went on for three months. We were both brooding in our neutral corners. Meanwhile, I decided to look around for a home. I called Jean, our real estate agent, and put her on the case. She showed me several charming houses, but I didn't really fall in love until, by describing a grand piano in the living room, she lured me into looking at a house in the lush rolling hills of Brentwood, a small township that dated back to the Civil War, about eleven miles from Nashville. It was love at first sight, a large three-level home incorporating wood, glass, and stone—open and modern. Light everywhere. The grounds were lovely. There was a pool and pool house. I thought I could be happy there. The price was steep but my royalties were good.

"Give me a few days to think about it," I told Jean.

During those few days, the phone rang. I was surprised to hear Waylon's voice.

"Jean took me to the house," he said, without even a trace of anger. He was as pleasant as could be.

"Oh, she did," I said.

"I like it. I think we should buy it."

That surprised me.

"Oh, you do," I said.

"I honestly do."

Neither of us mentioned our separation. There was no need to. The house seemed to symbolize a reconciliation. But was I willing? Seeking divine guidance, I fell to my knees in prayer. The answer came quickly. I felt that God would bless me if I left Waylon and also bless me if I stayed.

"But what do you want me to do?" I asked the Lord. When audible words didn't come, I struggled with the decision.

At one point, I spoke with my dear friend Addie, then married to a musician in Waylon's band, about my dilemma.

"He'll fall apart without you, Jessi," she said.

"I'm not sure about that."

"I am. And so is everyone else who knows Waylon. You're his rock. You're the one keeping him sane. Remember the time he thought bugs were crawling all over him and he insisted that the house be exterminated right there and then?"

It wasn't a pleasant memory. Waylon had been at the end of a bad pill binge and was seeing things.

"Well," said Addie, "you're the only one who could talk some sense into him."

"Maybe so," I said, "but I did call the exterminators."

"You know how to keep him calm."

"No one can keep Waylon calm."

"You're keeping him alive, Jessi. Your good influence, your positive energy, your connection to God—without your strength, he's lost."

Those words hit home.

My prayers intensified. And soon I clearly heard a voice inside say a single word: *stay*.

I didn't have to report the results of my deliberations to Waylon. Words weren't necessary. He understood. He wasn't looking for me to apologize to him about my zeal in demanding his conversion. I knew I was wrong and Waylon knew it too. Similarly, I wasn't looking for him to apologize to me about whatever nonsense he might have fallen into. He, too, was well aware of his own transgressions. The bottom line was obvious to us both: We'd seen that living apart wasn't working for us. We'd learned that we didn't want to break up. We wanted to be together. We loved each other dearly. And that was that.

I now admitted to myself that assuming spiritual leadership was neither wise nor necessary. Waylon was his own man. I was my own woman. I could be led by God without insisting that Waylon be led in the same way. My job was to love him absolutely. And absolute love requires compassion. That meant leaving my own set of assumptions so I could hear the stirrings of my lover's heart. I was learning that love means listening more than leading, understanding more than demanding.

We called our new home Southern Comfort because that's what it symbolized—a strong reconciliation and a new beginning. We saw it as our first honest-to-goodness, let's-live-here-forever home. It had the potential to be the kind of showplace—not gaudy, but distinctively beautiful—that, for all his success, Waylon had never lived in.

"The only problem," said Waylon, "is cash flow. Neil Reshen says we still owe the government back taxes. He says I don't have enough for the down payment. The present owner is demanding a large chunk in cash."

"Not to worry," I said. "My cash has been flowing rather nicely. I can provide the down payment."

Wisely, Waylon and I had retained separate banking accounts. His money might have been funny, but mine wasn't. My royalties for "I'm Not Lisa" were sitting in the bank. If buying this house was going to contribute to our happiness, as we both believed, then I was happy to fork over the funds.

I immediately went to work personalizing our home in ways that mirrored our sense of beauty. I worked with William F. Hamilton, a renowned decorator, who helped me augment the clean lines and modern elements with romantic fabrics, comfortable seating, and fabulous accessories. We selected antique tables and cabinets that reflected our storied surroundings. Southern Comfort was only a stone's throw away from the home of John Overton, advisor to Andrew Jackson. Before the Battle of Nashville during the Civil War, our Brentwood area had served as headquarters for John Hood of the Confederacy. We were encircled by history.

Even though I had let go of my insistence that Waylon follow my spiritual lead, I wasn't about to give up the faith I had recovered. It didn't matter that it didn't work for Waylon because it certainly did work for me.

My rekindled love for God was more than precious to me. It was motivational. It was the reason that, through these uncertain times with Waylon, I was able to go on. The part of myself that I had once discarded—the woman still known to my family as Mirriam—needed to introduce herself to the world. That meant releasing the *Mirriam* album.

Even though the music had been recorded and was ready to go, Capitol was still saying no. They were pleased that I was reaching both the country and pop markets. But, they argued, most artists switching from those fields to gospel wind up hurting their careers. I argued that I wasn't trying to redefine myself as a gospel artist. I simply had a suite of songs that were especially close to my heart. And my heart was saying, "Let this music be heard."

My reasoning, however, didn't convince the record company. Or Waylon.

"Honey, I hear you loud and clear," he said. "But I know this cold-hearted music business all too well. Even if you do put it out, I don't see Capitol promoting it."

"It's not about the promotion," I said. "It's about God. I'm gonna put it out there, Waylon. I really am."

"Far be it from me to mess with a hardheaded woman," he said good-naturedly. "You do what you gotta do."

And I did.

The album cover said "Jessi Colter" on top and "Mirriam" on the bottom. In between was a photograph of me in white. I used my new name—Jessi—because I had no intention of abandoning it. I was happy and proud of my success in secular music. There would be other secular albums to follow. But there would be no Jessi without Mirriam.

Mirriam was foundational to Jessi's spirit, and Mirriam needed to speak out. Mirriam needed to sing songs that reconnected her to her mother's church and her mother's faith.

"For Mama" was the first selection, followed by the songs I had been able to sing for her before she fell sick: "God, If I Could Only Write Your Love Song," "God, I Love You," "Let It Go," "I Belong to Him," and "There Ain't No Rain."

In the days before I made my irrevocable decision to release the record, I listened to it over and over again. Certain songs seemed more urgent, more expressive of my innermost devotion than ever. "I Belong to Him," for example, touched on both my relationship to Waylon and my relationship to God. I was delighted when Waylon and the great Roy Orbison agreed to sing the background vocals:

> A thousand ways, a thousand days
> The song of the world haunts a memory
>
> I played my part, it broke my heart
> But on the mend, I found a friend
>
> I belong to him

Other songs, like "Master, Master," were more traditional hymns in which, without other musical augmentation, I accompanied myself on piano. I sought the stark emotion of a simple prayer:

> Master, master, won't you touch me
> One touch can sanctify me
> The same hands we nailed to that old rugged cross
> Are the same hands that reach out to me

"Consider Me" considered my need and love for the living Christ:

He died a lonely man, he was the only one
I walked right through his door not knowing anymore
That I was ready for his gentle ways

I closed the album with "New Wine," a mysterious meditation that came to me in the form of fiddle-and-guitar sacred blues:

Here . . . now . . . seek . . . find . . . new
wine . . . from heaven

The new wine, of course, was my old new faith, restored and rechanneled through this album, *Mirriam*, that was finally released in 1977.

Unfortunately, Waylon's predictions proved all too accurate. Capitol had no interest in promoting it. Making matters worse, a change in management meant my champion in the marketing department had been replaced. The new exec was a numbers man with no feeling for a spiritual record. Certain it wouldn't catch on with the public, he buried it.

The dire predictions about my career, made by Waylon and Capitol, proved true. I never had another hit as popular as "I'm Not Lisa." And the sales of my following albums began to decline.

I hardly despaired. *Mirriam* was a record I had to make and share with the world. Even as I recognized the futility—and harm—in trying to control Waylon's spiritual path, I had to remain firmly on mine. If my career suffered, I did not. My relationship with God came first. My relationship with my family overshadowed my relationship to show business. I saw show business as fun, a less than serious way to sing songs and entertain people. Unlike Waylon, whose fierce dedication to his craft was unstoppable, I had no burning desire to set show business on fire.

In 1977, despite disappointing sales numbers for *Mirriam*, I was a happy woman. Jennifer was turning thirteen and had already developed a beautiful singing voice. Waylon was working away at Cowboy Jack Clement's studio, churning out platinum albums like *Ol' Waylon* and the aptly titled *I've Always Been Crazy*. His hair was getting longer, his beard was getting shaggier, and I liked the look.

On the cover of *Ol' Waylon*, the record that included his huge number-one hit with Willie—"Luckenbach, Texas"—he drew a red heart and wrote my name inside. I was touched. I was also delighted that *I've Always Been Crazy* included a medley of Buddy Holly songs, an indication that Waylon was at long last able to express in musical terms his abiding love for his mentor. On that same album he sang Shel Silverstein's endearing "Whistlers and Jugglers." The signature song, though, was Waylon's own "Don't You Think This Outlaw Bit's Done Got Out of Hand?"

The question came as the direct result of one of the worst episodes in Waylon's career. It was a week after Elvis died. On August 24, 1977, at Chips Moman's American Sound Studios in Nashville, while editing a Hank Williams Jr. version of my song "Storms Never Last," Waylon was hit by a storm he never saw coming.

He was busted for drugs.

Chapter 20

WHAT GOES AROUND COMES AROUND

The comforts of Southern Comfort, our beautiful new home, didn't last long. Our newfound domestic tranquility was turned inside out by Waylon's arrest.

I found out in a phone call.

"Honey," Waylon said, "I know this is gonna sound scary—and it is scary—but the Federal Drug Enforcement Agency is at the studio. There are eight agents and a bunch of local narcs and cops. They're searching this place with a fine-tooth comb and they may or may not come out to the house. I need you to go through all my things—I mean everything—and flush down the toilet anything that even looks suspicious. Do it now."

"Are you under arrest?" I asked.

"Don't think they're hauling me off tonight but can't be sure. I'll call when I can. But do what I ask, honey, and do it fast."

A dagger of fear pierced my heart. I ran to Waylon's closet and rifled through his stuff. Of course I knew he snorted cocaine. I even tried it once, just to understand what he found so alluring. I hated the feeling it gave me and I never touched it again. Waylon kept his stash far away from me. I had no idea where he hid it. All I knew was that I was looking for packets or vials of white powder. I searched the house—went through every drawer and article of his clothing—and found nothing. At about the time I had come up empty, he called again.

"I'm not coming home tonight," he said.

"Are you going to jail?" I asked, my heart in my throat.

"No. They haven't found anything, but they're still looking."

"So are they going to arrest you?"

"There'll be an arrest that probably won't stick. But it won't matter. The press already knows. It'll be all over the news tomorrow."

"If they're not taking you to jail, why don't you come home?"

"Reporters are gonna follow me. I don't want to get you entangled in this. I don't want them taking pictures of the house. It's best that I stay away until I can clear this up. You're gonna have to tell the kids something 'cause they're gonna hear about it at school."

Waylon was referring to my daughter Jennifer and his son Buddy.

"When will you be home?" I asked.

"Not for a while, hon," he said. "Not till I get a handle on this thing."

For the next few days, I felt like I was living inside a science fiction movie. I kept the kids out of school, which was wise, because, as Waylon predicted, the press had a field day. In newspapers across the country his fans read how he'd been arrested on alleged drug possession and faced up to fifteen years in prison.

The arrest did come, but he was able to post bond. Cautious to the point of paranoia, he stayed away from the house for weeks, living at the Hyatt in downtown Nashville, but he called every night to give me an update on the case. Naturally I was filled with fear. To read the newspaper accounts, my husband would soon be hauled off to federal prison.

Waylon kept reassuring me that wasn't going to happen. He kept telling everyone who worked with him that they should tell the truth and not try to protect him. Well, the truth was that Waylon had been using cocaine for years. He himself said he was a walking pharmacy.

But apparently he was able to get rid of all the drugs on him—plus all the drugs in the studio—before the agents started their search.

The case against him was built upon a package sent from Neil Reshen's office in New York to the studio. The Feds claimed that package was filled with cocaine. Waylon was certain one of his ex-wives had tipped off the Feds about the package. He hired a famous lawyer, Jay Goldberg, to handle the case. The legalities went on for months and cost us more than a hundred thousand dollars, but Goldberg was brilliant. He punched holes in the case, showing blatant defects in the government's faulty warrants.

Mark Rothbaum, who worked as an assistant for Neil, valiantly assumed blame for mailing the package and was sentenced to a very short term in a minimum-security facility. Willie Nelson was so impressed with Mark's loyalty that he hired him as his manager, a job that Mark maintains to this day, some forty years later. The end result for Waylon was that all charges were dropped.

In a weird way, all the hoopla surrounding the case increased Waylon's reputation as an outlaw. The music press, as well as his fans, ate it up. Big bad Waylon beat the Feds. His record sales went soaring. By this time, though, Waylon was fed up with the whole business—thus his song "Don't You Think This Outlaw Bit's Done Got Out of Hand?"

"I'm gonna presume this is enough to make you wanna stop," I said.

"It's not a bad presumption," said Waylon, "and right reason says it's the only sensible move."

"Then be sensible," I urged.

"Wish I could be. But I gotta be honest, and I honestly can't be making any promises to you I don't intend to keep."

Disheartened, I knew Waylon had no intention of quitting. All the bust did was make him more paranoid. He was convinced that our phones were tapped and our home was under surveillance. Though that was not the case, I realized the futility of trying to convince him otherwise. Waylon was more than headstrong. He was absolutely immovable when it came to change. He'd change when and only when he was ready.

Realizing that, I resigned myself to the fact that I was married to a man whose addiction would remain untreated as long as he chose. I saw my choice as twofold: I could stay and love him as best as I could, prayerfully nurturing him with patience and compassion, or I could leave him. I chose the former.

I suppose I could be seen as an enabler. I don't believe I was. I never pretended that my attitude about his drug habit was anything other than disgust. I never gave him the idea that it was okay with me. He understood to keep the drugs away from me. He honored the sanctity of our home. And at the next great crisis of my heart, he stood beside me, offering me the support I so badly needed. The crisis was the death of my father.

We were in London on one of those improbable side trips that characterized our lifestyle. In the aftermath of the legal nightmare, this project was a godsend—a concept album, a country-and-western opera called *White Mansions*, written by Paul Kennerley, an Englishman who'd composed a Civil War story seen through Southern eyes. When Kennerley heard Waylon's record of "That's Why Cowboys Sing the Blues," he decided that Waylon's voice was perfect to play the Drifter, a character who roamed the land, warning of the South's impending doom. I was cast as local plantation belle Polly Ann Stafford.

"It sounds a little weird," I'd told Waylon when he first explained the project to me.

"It's great, it's perfect."

"What makes you so sure?"

"Instinct. I feel it in my gut. Besides, it's being released by A&M,

Jerry Moss and Herb Alpert's label. They're the guys who signed me up before anyone knew my name. They're the true believers."

"All right. When are we leaving?"

"Day after tomorrow. Get to packing."

As I packed, I read over the lyrics and studied the story. Waylon was right. The songs were brilliant. Each character was imbued with compassion. I saw the narrative as a penetrating study of human empathy.

"Leave it to an Englishman to get it right," said Waylon. "We Americans are too close to our own history to see the forest from the trees."

We flew to London on the Concorde. Waylon sported a new pair of cowboy boots, a gift from an old bull-rider friend. But the boots were a size too small, and when we got to our fancy hotel overlooking Grosvenor Square, it took a three-hundred-pound security man to pull them off Waylon's swollen feet. His feet were so sore he had to walk into the recording studio barefoot.

That's when we met Glyn Johns, the man who'd produced the Beatles, the Rolling Stones, Bob Dylan, and The Who—just to name a few. Glyn brought in, among others, Eric Clapton and the Ozark Mountain Daredevils. The music was riveting, soulful, and deep.

When we got back to the hotel after the first day, Waylon was the most animated I'd seen him in months. He loved how the English writer interpreted the Civil War without bias, dramatizing the bigotry and brutality on both sides. Waylon especially appreciated the subtlety of his character, a troubadour who walked the line between the North and South and understood that the real villain wasn't a region but war itself.

Because he was a Southerner—and also because our new Nashville home was situated in the middle of Civil War history—Waylon took *White Mansions* personally and ranked it among his favorite albums.

One of the songs I sang that moved me most expressed Polly's feelings for the wounded men facing death. What I didn't know—the news Waylon wanted to spare me until we were through recording— was that at that precise moment back home in Arizona, my own father was dying from pneumonia.

Waylon and I flew home to Mesa as quickly as we could. My brother Johnny said that Daddy's passage had been peaceful. He told how, just before his passing, Daddy sat up in bed and sang a corny old song he used to croon to Mother whenever she'd scold him for discussing money at the dinner table and called him "Carnal Arnold."

"I love you so much," he'd sing, "it hurts me . . . I love you . . . I love you . . ."

We buried him in a plot next to the woman who saw how he'd been slain in the Spirit, curing his throat cancer and enabling him to live a long life of ceaseless exploration and endless optimism. He had loved me unconditionally. He had also loved Waylon, who looked to him as a second father. I cherish the times Waylon went to the mine with Daddy and spent days listening to his war stories of prospecting in the Arizona wilderness.

In his relationship to Mother, Daddy had shown me what it means for a man to respect a woman. He encouraged her to lead her life as a disciple of God, both separate from their diverse pursuits yet joined in the spirit. Together they had served their muses—hers was Jesus, his natural science—without trampling on each other. I am blessed to be their progeny, a product of their miraculous marriage. They live in my heart today, as they always will.

When your parents die, that invisible wall that has appeared to protect you from alien elements seems to fall. Your sense of vulnerability sharpens. You are left alone. You feel a sadness you have never felt before.

I felt all those things. Yet the feeling I remember most wasn't one of fear but rather one of gratitude. It was my parents who taught me to face fear with equanimity. It was my parents who taught me to walk through fear. They exemplified courage. They exemplified perseverance.

Thus I persevered. I persevered through the challenges of a professional and personal life that became, all at once, as exciting as it was complex.

---— Chapter 21 ---—

A COWBOY ROCKS
AND ROLLS

"How do you feel 'bout doing a rock-and-roll record?" asked Waylon one morning during a late breakfast at Southern Comfort.

"I feel great. Why would I feel otherwise?"

"Don't know. Just thinking you might wanna make another gospel record. Don't wanna be accused of stifling Mirriam."

"Mirriam can't be stifled," I said. "And besides, she's delighted with the gospel record she made. In time she'll make another. But I can assure you that Jessi has no problem rocking and rolling."

"That's my girl."

Waylon had a bunch of songs written by great writers that he wanted me to hear. Over the course of several days, we listened to them all. I began to envision the project as a joyful dance record, a welcome antidote to the challenging times Waylon and I had recently endured.

One in particular—"That's the Way a Cowboy Rocks and Rolls"—was written by our friend Tony Joe White and seemed especially apt as an album title. Growing up in Arizona, I'd long been fascinated by cowboy culture and saw, as did Waylon, a direct correlation between the rough-and-ready western hero and his rock counterpart. They both stood outside the mainstream; they both were always moving on, living a vagabond life against a backdrop of some enticing romantic dream. The dream was elusive, and the search for the ultimate roundup or the lost chord never stopped.

There were songs by Johnny Cash ("A Cowboy's Last Ride") and Neil Young ("Hold Back the Tears"). I didn't at all object to singing an album of covers rather than originals. I was delighted to work as an interpretive singer instead of as a writer. "Black Haired Boy," Guy Clark's poignant literary portrait of an enigmatic youngster, remains one of my favorite recordings. Waylon's favorite, "Maybe You Should've Been Listening (When I Said Goodbye)" contains an achingly beautiful steel guitar solo by Ralph Mooney, a legendary musician who, like drummer Richie Albright, had been a Waylor—a member of Waylon's formidable band—for decades. Waylon considered Mooney a genius.

Together with Richie, Waylon produced the album. As a supervisor, Waylon had a gentle and supportive touch. I marveled at his mastery in the studio. I saw him as a musical architect. Though he could neither read nor write music, he could construct sturdy compositions as well as complex arrangements. He was totally committed to his craft.

The final song, written by Donnie Fritts and Spooner Oldham, was "Oh, My Goodness." I heard it as a prayer—and a fitting one at that. Its simple message underlines the need for gratitude for the goodness that exists in this mean ol' world. I believe that the only path to joy is through gratitude. How else can joy be realized on a consistent basis? Without the conscious cultivation of gratitude, we fall into negativity and despair. Choosing gratitude is a decision that requires effort. The effort is worth it because the payoff is beautiful. The payoff is joy.

As the seventies wound down, some ten years into my marriage to Waylon, I recommitted myself to gratitude. I required gratitude. It would have been easy—far too easy—to fall into resentment.

Stubborn as a mule, Waylon continued to pop his pills and snort his coke. In the meantime, I thought of the old cliché "If you want to hold on, you have to let go." I did want to hold on. I remained convinced that one day—and soon—the man I loved would face and defeat his demons. I was grateful for the knowledge that for him to do just that, I'd have to let go. I couldn't be bugging him. I couldn't be trying to control him. I knew better than to give him ultimatums. I'd have to grind it out through gratitude. Gratitude for the excitement Waylon had brought to my life. Gratitude for the power of our physical and spiritual love. Gratitude for the patience God was granting me day by day.

Thinking positively, I looked around and saw so much to be grateful for. I absolutely loved the extraordinary people I had met through Waylon—particularly June and Johnny Cash and Connie and Willie Nelson. Remarkable individuals all, these were friends of the heart. Some—like Johnny and George Jones—danced with many of the same devils that had seduced Waylon. Nonetheless I found them fascinating.

Duane had first introduced me to George, who along with Don Gibson had initially converted me to the beauty of country music. George would often drop by Southern Comfort. He adored Waylon and even gave him an 18-karat gold horseshoe-shaped ring set with diamonds. Waylon thought George Jones was the greatest singer in the history of country music but also said, "He's got more complexes than anybody I've ever met. If you can believe it, he's insecure about his singing."

Maybe that's why George drank so much. When he showed up at our doorstep, he was usually high. One time he nearly tore up our living room—I never did know why—until Waylon literally tied him up. Another time he wouldn't leave until I went to the piano and sang "Darlin' It's Yours"—not once, but four times in a row.

Waylon's relationship with George was much like his relationship with Johnny and Willie: brothers to the bone. It was Waylon who helped George through a rough patch of tax problems. Later, when George was flush, he gifted Waylon a vintage 1927 Ford coupe. We knew George before he met Nancy—the love of his life—and after. He was much easier to deal with after.

Waylon succinctly summed up George when, referring to his hometown, he said, "George Jones is pure Vidor, Texas, 1958."

Another lovable and incorrigible character, Hank Williams Jr., became Waylon's little brother. They spent long days and nights in each other's company, exploring the deep mythology attached to Hank's father and philosophizing, as country singers are inclined to do, about the meaning of it all.

I loved listening to their duet on "The Conversation," a song they wrote together in which Waylon says, "Hank, let's talk about your daddy, tell me how your mama loved that man," and Hank answers, "Well, just break out a bottle, hoss, and I'll tell you 'bout the driftin' cowboy band."

In short, for all its insomnia-induced insanity, I was grateful to be part of Waylon's world. Not a dull day, not an uneventful evening. The action was ongoing and, best of all, the creativity was supercharged.

My gratitude reached even higher ground when, in September 1978, I learned I was pregnant. This was the result of deep deliberation and careful planning. It was important to Waylon that we have a child together. The clock was ticking. He was forty-one, I was thirty-five. We loved his teenagers from his previous marriages, just as we loved Jennifer. Terry, Julie, Buddy, Deana, and Tomi Lynne—all wonderful people with unique personalities and special talents. We were blessed to have them in our lives. And yet Waylon knew that, given the difficult and complex circumstances surrounding his broken marriages, he had never been able to realize his full potential as a father.

"If I die without having a shot at being a truly good dad," he said, "I'll feel like a heel. And the only way that's gonna happen, honey, is if you and I conceive a child of our own."

I had reservations. It wasn't because my love for Waylon had diminished. If anything, my love had grown. I was worried that his drug use would negatively affect the embryo. Twice I went to the doctor to have my IUD removed and twice I crawled off the table before the birth control device could be removed. I simply wasn't sure. When I asked God for guidance, that still, silent voice I'd learned to trust led me to Isaiah 53:5: "He was wounded for our transgressions, He was bruised for our iniquities; the chastisement for our peace was upon Him, and by His stripes we are healed."

This wasn't the passage I wanted to read. I wanted a passage that would indicate an unambiguous yes or no. So I kept asking God and kept being redirected to Isaiah 53:5. The passage wouldn't leave me alone.

"Why, Lord," I asked, "can't you be any clearer?"

The relevance of the passage did not come quickly. It took me a long while to grasp what God was saying: "Don't worry, my child. I have carried your sins. I have carried your husband's sins. I have carried the sins of the world. I was bruised for your iniquities but my love was not."

Christ's suffering—the bruising of his physical body, the torture he had endured—led to his victory over death. And because he has risen, we, too, can rise above our own sicknesses, whether of the body or the soul.

I asked Waylon whether he would take my hand and let me pray. He agreed.

"If it is your will to give us a child, Father God, give this child the very best of both of us."

A month later, I learned I was pregnant.

Ironically, I had no strange cravings while, for his part, Waylon suddenly was compelled to eat great fistfuls of licorice jelly beans night and day. It was hardly news that my husband had an addictive personality.

Nine months rolled by without incident. I worked and traveled normally. I was careful to get good sleep and diligently kept up my standard of what I considered stylish dress. My pregnancy was hardly visible until the final three months.

Then came Saturday, May 19, 1979. I could feel that the birth was imminent and asked Waylon to drive me to Nashville Baptist Hospital. June Carter Cash was already there, waiting to keep us company. Johnny was on his way. To pass the time, Waylon and I decided to play a game of spades, placing the cards on my stomach. It was an amusing diversion.

"Out in West Texas where my other kids were born," said Waylon, "men weren't allowed in the delivery room. Here, they are."

My water broke, the contractions intensified, and we were off to the races.

"I'd better run out for some cigarettes," said Waylon.

"If you go," I pleaded, "you'll miss this."

"All right, I'll stay."

A young male junior nurse was busy arranging the room when he noticed Johnny Cash standing in the hall. Thrilled, he rushed out to greet him.

When he returned, I was in the full throes of predelivery pain.

"Oh, my God, Johnny Cash is out there," the nurse breathlessly exclaimed. "He wants you to know he's here. It's actually him! It's actually Johnny Cash in person!"

He wouldn't shut up about it until I finally said, "Someone give this poor child a dime so he can call someone who gives a hoot about him seeing Johnny Cash—'cause I'm in here trying to have a baby."

With Waylon on the verge of passing out, the baby emerged a few minutes later, a beautiful dark-haired boy.

Waylon Albright Jennings.

He was placed on my stomach where only a few hours earlier Waylon had dealt an ace of spades.

Because I didn't like the idea of referring to my husband as Big Waylon and my son as Little Waylon, I thought of a western nickname that would fit nicely into our family lore: Shooter.

The name stuck. Shooter had arrived, a blessing in ways we could not yet know. Two months later, Waylon and I sent out an invitation:

IF YOU'VE EVER BEEN IN LOVE
WE WOULD LIKE TO INVITE YOU TO SHARE OUR JOY
AS MAGNOLIAS, MOONLIGHT, AND A CANDLELIGHT DINNER
SET THE STAGE FOR THE CHRISTENING OF
WAYLON ALBRIGHT JENNINGS
ON WEDNESDAY, THE TWENTY-FIFTH OF JULY
8 PM AT OUR HOME.
BRING LOVE, THANKSGIVING, AND BE READY
FOR A NIGHT TO REMEMBER.
WAYLON AND JESSI

I went all out. Our backyard was blooming with white caladiums, white mums, and white impatiens with tender ferns—all planted just for the celebration. A huge white tent was set up on our tennis court. Magnolias were floating on our pool. And then came the rains. From morning on, it poured all day, nonstop, until the clock struck eight. Just like that, the rain stopped as the guests arrived to the lyrical strains of classical music provided by a string quartet.

Among the many guests was Muhammad Ali, who'd been introduced to Waylon years before by Kris Kristofferson. "I've never seen two people so taken with each other," Kris had told me. Muhammad, whose courage and integrity Waylon greatly admired, remained one of my husband's closest friends.

Of course June and Johnny were there along with manager Neil Reshen and attorney Jay Goldberg, who'd flown in from New York.

We asked Will D. Campbell, a Baptist minister, to preside over the christening. Born in Mississippi, Brother Will was a prominent advocate for civil rights—one of the four adults who escorted the black children integrating the Little Rock public schools in 1957, and the only caucasian present at the founding of the Southern Christian Leadership Conference by Dr. Martin Luther King Jr.

A tireless antiwar activist, Will had become a dear family friend and one of the few men of the cloth Waylon took to. I'd met the minister years earlier when Johnny Darrell, famous for singing "With Pen in Hand," invited Waylon and me to his wedding, held inside Will's one-room log cabin outside Nashville. There must have been forty people squeezed into this rural cabin, empty except for a bed, a desk that held an old manual typewriter, and a stove where a pot of black-eyed peas was cooking. Will spoke with striking simplicity and humility. He reminded me of Mother.

During the christening I held my baby in my arms with Waylon standing on my right. As the ceremony proceeded, Shooter started to wail. With every eye on me, I tried every trick in the book to calm him down. No such luck.

"Give him to me," said Waylon, with self-assurance.

The minute Shooter slipped into Waylon's powerful arms, he fell silent, a telling omen of what would evolve into a remarkable father-son relationship.

For all the joy brought forth by Shooter's birth, problems remained—problems chiefly predicated by Waylon's headstrong refusal, in spite of the dramatic drug bust, to put down his hurtful behavior.

The burning question I was too afraid to answer was inescapable:

Will Waylon ever find the strength to destroy his drugs before they destroy him?

Part Four

THE RECONCILIATION

Chapter 22

FLYING HIGH, FALLING LOW

A FRIEND RECENTLY REFERRED ME TO THOMAS MERTON, THE Trappist monk and author of the spiritual memoir *The Seven Storey Mountain*. In that book, Merton imagines living in a land where Christ would direct all things, where Merton's connection to God "would be as if he thought with my mind, as if he willed with my will." He speaks of the living Christ dwelling within his heart, "melting me into himself in the fires of his love."[1]

These words remind me of my prayers as I continued to live with—and to fervently love—a man who still had not completely found himself. I did understand why—or at least I thought I did. Waylon had never known a day without hard work. He'd started out working the fields when he was ten. In one way or another, he'd never stopped working those fields. All the drugs did was fuel his work ethic to a feverish pitch. Because of his hardscrabble life, I don't believe Waylon felt worthy of God's love.

"Grace isn't anything you earn," I told him. "It's a given. It's a gift."

He looked at me and smiled. He didn't argue, but I don't think he understood. The concept of unmerited favor—especially unmerited divine favor—had no concrete parallel in Waylon's world. In the world of show business, you scratched and clawed for every victory. You cut records, one after another, month after month, year after year. You toured endlessly. You promoted excessively. The grind was relentless. And when you did achieve success, you couldn't help but see it as a result of some herculean effort on your part.

In the late seventies and early eighties, in spite of—or partly because of—the sensational publicity surrounding Waylon, he was insulated by unprecedented success. The harder he worked, the more wrong he did, the greater his rewards. He was caught in a self-perpetuating cycle that was too insidious for anyone—even a wife—to shut down.

For seven long seasons he was the narrator on one of the most popular TV shows ever—*The Dukes of Hazzard*—for which he wrote and sang the theme song, "Good Ol' Boys," which became a huge hit on its own. He kept turning out hit albums like *Ol' Waylon*, *What Goes Around Comes Around*, *Music Man*, and *Black on Black* that in turn generated hit singles like "I Ain't Living Long Like This" and "Luckenbach, Texas," a town, ironically enough, Waylon had never seen.

What Waylon did see, though, was an increasingly adoring public willing to follow him wherever he went. He and Willie became the Lou Gehrig and Babe Ruth of country music, teammates on an undefeatable squad of champions. Beyond Willie, he sang duets with all the reigning legends—George Jones and he sang "Night Life"; Johnny Cash and he sang "There Ain't No Good Chain Gang"; Kris Kristofferson and he sang "Chase the Feeling"; Neil Diamond and he sang "One Good Love."

Like any hardworking artist, he reveled in his triumphs. And, true to his generous heart, he insisted that I share in the success. He was insistent that, after *That's the Way a Cowboy Rocks and Rolls*, he produce another Jessi Colter record. It was another spirited effort. We called it *Ridin' Shotgun*, and it included a song I wrote with Basil McDavid, "Holdin' On"—an accurate two-word synopsis of my marriage to Waylon—and one I wrote for and sang with my daughter

Jennifer, who had grown into a beautiful seventeen-year-old with a gorgeous voice.

This time around my original compositions—like "Ain't Making No Headlines (Here Without You)" and "Hard Times and Sno-Cone"— were more whimsical than reflective. Maybe that's because, unlike in an earlier period of our relationship, I'd made my peace with Waylon. Come what may, I was in it for the long haul.

Knowing my commitment, Waylon lent further support to my career by insisting that we release a duet album, *Leather and Lace*. The big hit off the record—and the composition of mine that has been covered more than any other—was our version of "Storms Never Last," the same song I had sung on my first Capitol LP seven years earlier. I loved singing with Waylon. Our harmony was as natural as a sunrise.

In 1981, I decided to throw Waylon a big surprise forty-fourth birthday bash. I wanted it to be a royal occasion and worked up a country-western theme. Once again, we tented the backyard, but this time erected a stage where bluegrass music would be provided by virtuosos Billy and Terry Smith. Guests were told to arrive in full western gear.

I thought my plan was perfect, since Waylon wouldn't be returning to town until 8:00 p.m., just in time for the big surprise. But Waylon, being Waylon, strolled in at 3:00 p.m., looked around at the army of caterers and asked, "Where's my party?"

"What party?" was my lame reply.

The game was up but that night the party was on. The guest list included Hank Williams Jr., LeAnn and Tony Joe White, minister Will Campbell, and, as a special surprise, one of Waylon's childhood heroes—Ernest Tubb and his Texas Troubadours. The barbecue brisket, ribs, and chicken were sizzlin'. The music was so hot we all got to dancing. Little Jimmy Dickens, then the oldest member of the Grand Ole Opry, was the most outlandishly dressed in his bright orange rhinestone suit and matching orange Stetson. If I do say so myself, my purple getup was pretty dazzling. Shooter, who had turned two, was outfitted to look like a miniature Waylon. Big Waylon had a ball.

I wasn't without worry, but I was able to live a life in which I staunchly supported my husband. Yes, I fretted about his health. Yes, I saw his habit of going days without sleep as deeply injurious. Yes, I was frightened by what he was doing to his body. Yes, I wanted to intervene, I wanted to scream, I wanted to take control, I wanted to insist that he turn his life over to the love of Christ, I wanted to cajole and threaten and demand. I desperately wanted to change him. But, in the end, I knew I couldn't. All I could do was love him. And if love, as Jesus promises, is the most powerful force of all, I could do no more and no less than lean on love.

It wasn't much later that I started working on what I considered the best of my rock-and-roll records. This one was called *Rock and Roll Lullaby*, named for a song by Barry Mann and Cynthia Weil. The album was put together by maestro Chips Moman and his piano player partner Bobby Emmons.

Chips had just produced the brilliant *Black on Black* album for Waylon. I was crazy about the guy. His real name is Lincoln, but, given his gambling prowess, he goes by Chips. He has these extra-wide eyes and the face of a duck—a handsome duck but a duck all the same.

Chips first approached Waylon about producing me.

"I think it's best if you weren't around when we record," Chips told Waylon.

"Why is that?" Waylon wanted to know.

"Because Jessi will look to you for direction."

"And is that a problem, hoss?"

"It is," said Chips, "if I'm the one in charge."

"When it comes to Jessi," said Waylon, "she's the one who's really in charge. She'll just fool you into thinking you are."

So with Waylon's approval, Chips came to me with a proposal at the same time my Capitol contract was up. It was a difficult decision. Columbia had offered me a deal that would have prevented Chips from producing. That's because Chips, along with his business partners Phil Walden and Buddy Killen, had formed Triad Records. They wanted me to sign exclusively with them.

"What do you think?" I asked Waylon.

"Your guess is as good as mine. Musically, no one's better than Chips. But in terms of worldwide distribution, no one's bigger than Columbia."

My decision was to put the music first. I signed with Chips.

"Glad to have you on board," said Chips, "but let me pick the material I think is right for you. I know you're a great writer—and I love your songs—but I want to feature your singing. What do you say?"

I said yes.

The sessions took place at Chips's Nashville studio, one of the best in the country. Everything fell smoothly into place. I was thrilled to sing songs like "Wild and Blue," "I'm Going by Daydream," and especially "I Can't Stop Loving You," written by Don Gibson, one of my early songsmith heroes. There's something about that Chips Moman sound, cultivated in his own American Studios, that made me want to sing all night long. Chips put together his usual crackerjack unit of top-flight players and, if you can believe it, even caved in when I suggested that Waylon sit in on guitar. The record could not have turned out better. Musically, I made the right decision. On the business side, though, I made a mistake.

A month or so after the album was ready for distribution—the cover showed me in short hair and a denim vest—Chips came roaring over to Southern Comfort on his Harley. I invited him in and asked if he'd like some coffee.

"Sure thing," he said, "but I'd better give you the bad news first."

"What's wrong?" I asked.

"Phil Walden and I had a falling out."

"Which means?"

"Your record's not coming out."

"Why in the world not?"

"We're folding the label."

"Even before you get started?"

"Afraid so."

"Well, I still love the music."

"Me too," said Chips. "I count it among my best productions."

Today the LP exists only as a rare collector's item. Naturally I wish more people could have heard it, but I don't regret making it. I hold on to the hope that one day soon it will be rescued from dark obscurity and see the light of day.

The softening of my career came at a time that was not displeasing to me. Jennifer was a teenager and Shooter a toddler. They needed my undivided attention, and I was grateful to grant them just that. The path that I was following—allowing Waylon to follow his own path in his own way—always led back to the Lord.

I read in Psalm 150:

> Praise God in his sanctuary: praise him in
>   the firmament of his power.
> Praise him for his mighty acts: praise him
>   according to his excellent greatness.
> Praise him with the sound of the trumpet: praise
>   him with the psaltery and harp.
> Praise him with the timbrel and dance: praise him
>   with stringed instruments and organs.
> Praise him upon the loud cymbals: praise him
>   upon the high sounding cymbals.
> Let every thing that hath breath praise the
>   LORD. Praise ye the LORD. (KJV)

God was telling me to praise him—not because he needed praise but because the very act of perpetual praise liberated me from self-concern and preoccupation with Waylon.

I praised God for every day, for every breath, for every good thought that came my way. Mostly, though, I praised God for informing my heart of the very concept of praise. Without shouting his praise, whether silently or out loud in the full-gospel glory of the Greater Apostolic Christ Church, I'd never have been able to get past the brambles and thorns of fear and despair.

Chapter 23

PATIENCE

It was 1984. We'd been married nearly fifteen years. My spiritual life had become increasingly independent. My prayers were consistent.

Touch him, dear Lord, as you have touched me. Pierce his heart as you have pierced mine.

But even as I prayed those urgent desires, I knew that the ultimate prayer still had to be for patience. In my willfulness, I wanted God to touch Waylon *now*, to pierce his heart *today*.

I had to repeat the same prayerful mantra: "The Lord might not be there when you want him, but he's always right on time."

His timing, not mine.

His will, not mine.

His grace, his mercy, his mystery, his wisdom.

That wisdom led me back to the fact that compassion, if fully realized, always allows for greater patience.

During the Christmas season of 1983, Johnny Cash's family staged a successful intervention. Johnny, whose drug dependence was as severe as Waylon's, agreed to go to the Betty Ford Center in California.

Bill Robinson, a close business associate of Waylon's manager, came to me with the idea of a similar intervention. Waylon's health had been dramatically deteriorating. Suffering from laryngitis, he had missed several gigs. He looked bedraggled. He was deeply depressed. His insomnia was off the charts. Wouldn't it be best if the family confronted him with the truth of his desperate condition?

My anxious mind said yes, but my spirit said no. I knew Waylon as well as any woman can know a man. Waylon Jennings wasn't Johnny Cash. I could see how Johnny, a believing Christian, might accept himself as a broken man requiring help. But Waylon was different. Call it a steely stubborn streak. Call it an uncommonly strong sense of self. The terms don't matter, but the reality did. Waylon's emotional reality was such that no outside influence could persuade him to do what he himself had not decided to do on his own. I concluded that an intervention would do more harm than good.

I had to wait. And wait. And wait some more.

I believe Shooter had much to do with Waylon's ultimate decision to give up drugs. In one instance, Waylon discovered Shooter taking a straw and inserting it in his nose, clearly imitating his father. It was an act that devastated Waylon, who described it to me with tears in his eyes. Yet even after that incident, I knew I couldn't push Waylon. I had to wait.

The first indication that the wait might be over came in March 1984 when Waylon came out and said, "I'm not going to quit, I'm just going to stop."

"Fine," I said.

"I'll stop for a month. What do you think?"

"I think you need to figure this out in your own way and on your own terms. You're a smart man, Waylon. You know yourself. If this is your plan, I'm with you."

"I'm also thinking of us going out to Arizona. If I'm gonna stop, it's gonna be easier to stop there."

To be honest, I felt some trepidation about the trip. There had been a number of other attempts to come off drugs that had been less than successful. Once we'd gone to Malibu where we rented a house on the beach. As always, Waylon's intentions were good. The weather was ideal, the coast peaceful and calm. I stayed in prayer. And for a while Waylon stayed sober. But once back to reality and the grind of the road, he succumbed. That broke my heart. While I would always support Waylon's attempt to break free of his addiction, I was afraid of building up too much hope. No matter, I agreed to accompany Waylon, making him extremely happy.

"Arizona's always been good to me, baby," he said. "It's where I met you. It's where I went out on those great trips to your daddy's mine. I feel a peace in Arizona I don't feel anywhere else. I think it's the desert. The desert is deep. The desert leaves it up to you. And this time I think I can do it."

After canceling all our gigs, Waylon, Shooter, and I rode on the tour bus from Nashville to Paradise Valley outside Phoenix. We had no plans. All we had was a rented house stocked with food. It was a glorious time of year to be in the desert. The cloudless sky was a blanket of blue. The air was clean. The jagged rocks, the flowering cacti, the audacious mountains were exciting and calming all at the same time.

March 31, a few days after we arrived, Waylon went to the bus where I knew he had a big stash of cocaine.

I wanted to say, "No, this last binge might kill you! If you wanna stop, stop now! Stop this very minute! You're being foolish! You're being headstrong! Come to your senses before it's too late!"

Instead, I said nothing. Waylon went to the bus. That night I couldn't sleep. When he came in the next morning, he looked like death warmed over.

"I didn't do it all," he said. "I left twenty thousand dollars' worth of cocaine on the bus."

"Shouldn't you destroy it?" I asked.

"I just wanna leave it there."

"Is that really smart?"

"It's not smart, but it's what I wanna do."

I didn't argue. I wasn't there to argue. I was just there to be a loving presence.

Later, reflecting on the ordeal, Waylon told me that he couldn't handle the withdrawal without having what he called an escape hatch. Yet he did handle it. The ordeal was painful both physically and emotionally. He said every bone in his body screamed out in anguish.

In his autobiography, I was deeply moved to read his description of those difficult days and his concern for me:

> I'd sit out on the swing in the front yard, watching the sun come up. I'd still be there when the stars began to shine. As my mind started to clear, I got to seeing the look on Jessi's face. It was hopeless and helpless. She was so sad, watching me vacillate between life and death, unable to do more than watch me go through it. . . . I slowly learned how to feel my emotions again. . . . I woke up one morning, toward the end [of withdrawal], and Jessi was sitting there by the end of the bed. . . .
>
> "Jessi, my spirit's dying and there's nothing I can do about it."
>
> There wasn't anything she could do but wait, pray in her fashion, and let me know that she was holding fast, right by my side. I couldn't have done it without Jessi. She is the most giving person I've ever met, and anytime I felt like I just couldn't stand withdrawing further, she let me know, by her gentle presence, what would be waiting for me on life's other shore.[1]

We rode back to Nashville where, in Waylon's words, Southern Comfort became his own "halfway house." I was thrilled when he asked me to play old hymns on the grand piano in our living room. I played them for hours on end. Waylon just sat there, his eyes closed. On other afternoons he'd watch Shooter play in the front yard.

Sometimes we'd go for rides. During one of those rides, he said, referring to one of his closest friends, "Have you told him I quit?"

That was the first time he'd used the word *quit*.

"You realize what you've just said, don't you?" I asked.

"I said I quit."

"Before you were saying you'd just stopped. You've never said 'quit' before."

"Well, I said it now."

"And you mean it?"

"Wouldn't have said it if I didn't mean it."

That night Waylon went out to the bus and brought back a suitcase that he handed to me.

"What's this?"

"Twenty thousand dollars' worth of you-know-what."

"And what am I supposed to do with it?"

"Dump it."

I went to the toilet, poured it out, and flushed it down.

"What do you have to say now?" he asked me.

"Hallelujah!"

Waylon maintained his sobriety for the rest of his life, but the immediate aftermath wasn't easy.

He had nightmares and struggled with his weight. He talked about the loss of his alter ego—the good-time Charlie, he called him—the man who was convinced he was nothing without cocaine. He viewed the death of good-time Charlie with a mixture of alarm, regret, and relief. It was a confusing time.

The fact that Waylon never again laid out another line is credit to the strength of his character. Beyond that strength, though, Shooter was another powerful motivator, another reason Waylon found the wherewithal to stay sober.

One of the poignant pictures that Waylon painted in his book focused on our son: "I was sitting with Shooter in a restaurant booth.

He was on the inside, and he got his coloring book out. He was all of five years old. He put his left arm through my right, and we sat there for about an hour while he colored. Shooter hadn't ever done that before. I'd never been able to sit so still for so long with him. I wasn't about to remove my arm."[2]

On the humorous side, Waylon's protective attitude about Shooter could get out of hand. There was the time when a snake was spotted in a section of our yard where Shooter liked to play. Waylon became convinced that the only way to safeguard our son from dangerous reptiles was to buy a herd of pigs, since pigs are known to eat snakes. He had Maureen Rafferty, our ever-loyal assistant, running all over town trying to find hogs for sale. Fortunately, Waylon eventually dropped the idea, although his concern for Shooter's welfare never diminished.

In heroic fashion, Waylon was able to white-knuckle his way through to the other side and live a sober life. Not everyone is capable of such a feat. I have friends who owe their lives to twelve-step programs like Alcoholics Anonymous and Cocaine Anonymous. I know those programs are based on the acceptance of a higher power who can do for us what we can't do for ourselves. I applaud those programs.

Other friends, like Johnny Cash, have found therapeutic modalities, like the ones offered at Betty Ford, to be lifesaving blessings. I have nothing but admiration for rehabilitation centers run by well-trained professionals with a heart for healing. Some addicts are slain in the Spirit of God and, just like that, their addictions are lifted. I witnessed such miracles in my mother's church. The paths to recovery are many. The path one chooses is a highly individual choice that may not be right for everyone.

Waylon chose the most difficult path. He went to the desert where he set out his temptations and faced them down. I believe he was sincere when he wrote that my presence was a help. But in this epic struggle, I was an observer not a participant. The struggle pitted

Waylon against himself. In a scenario where most men would fail, he prevailed.

Let me be plain: I do not consider Waylon's way to sobriety as a template for others. I would never encourage anyone to rely, as he did, on sheer willpower. That's usually a recipe for disaster.

I thank God that Waylon made it work. I thank God that I knew enough to stay out of his way. And I thank God that Waylon, whether due to his rugged individualism or headstrong constitution, had enough self-regard to choose life over death. It was a miraculous moment when Waylon's will and the will of God finally met.

Chapter 24

TIME TO PARTY

I ALWAYS LOVED HOSTING SOPHISTICATED THEME PARTIES THAT celebrated milestones. But a sobriety party was something entirely new.

The first sobriety party was hosted by June Carter Cash for Waylon at their mansion on Old Hickory Lane. It was a small affair with a few friends like actor Robert Duvall, himself an aspiring country singer and songwriter. June and Johnny each sang songs they had written to celebrate Waylon's sobriety.

At that party Johnny took me aside to ask, "Jessi, do you think you could give me a party like this?"

I thought his request both funny and touching—funny because there was always a very mild brotherly rivalry between Johnny and Waylon, and touching because Johnny was so sincere in his request. When Waylon came out of the Arizona desert and went through his long drying-out period, he had often called Johnny.

"Of course I'll throw you a party," I told Johnny.

"I was hoping you'd say that," he said.

I got the party-planning fever and decided on a fifties theme. I thought everyone would enjoy re-imagining a more innocent era when we were all a lot less world-weary. With the help of our endlessly resourceful assistant Maureen, who had a great imagination and love of celebration, things quickly fell into place. It was an afternoon picnic-on-the-grounds affair, casual except for me in my yellow-netted strapless prom dress and Waylon in his midnight-black prom tux. Johnny arrived wearing jeans and a T-shirt with a pack of cigarettes rolled up in his sleeve. June wore an aqua taffeta and lace gown, a perfect example of midcentury fashion. Robert Duvall came dressed up as June and his wife Gail dressed up as Johnny. He later led the hilarious ceremony that roasted the man of the hour.

Kris and Lisa Kristofferson, along with their firstborn, Jesse, flew in from California as surprise guests. I was so delighted that everyone showed up—Becky and Hank Williams, Connie and Willie Nelson, plus Rodney Crowell who led the sing-along.

The sobriety theme in no way diminished the joy of the party. Everyone stayed late into the night. We danced and laughed and joked and sang. I can't remember a more fun-loving evening. The high point—at least for me—came the next afternoon when Johnny showed up at our door and hand delivered this letter.

Dear Jessi, the newness of life, which Waylon and I are experiencing, was promised us in Romans 8:13, "If you live by the flesh, you shall die, but if, through the spirit, you mortify the deeds of the body, you shall live." Mortify means to make dead. For us and our death-dealing habits, there had to be death. He who said, "I am the way, the truth and the life" has triumphed in that through your prayers and all our perseverance, we have made dead the old man in us and now we have become heirs to the promise of life through Him. I ask you to take note of where Waylon and I are now. We are milk-fed babies in the spirit. Even with my background and this being my second time around, I am in no higher spiritual plane than Waylon, possibly, not as high, because he is in the joy of first discovery of spiritual truths. I thank you for your prayers, but

I ask you to continue to pray along with Dulcie and others for our wisdom and discretion. For in God's battles, even as in the U.S. Marines, discretion is still the better part of valor. Pray for our wisdom and know that I hold you in highest esteem and love you as a sister in Him. You have ministered to my spiritual needs as no man or woman has done in a long, long time. Last night your home was filled, overflowing with His bountiful love—and that it was directed at me makes me tremble. Thank you and God bless you, your brother, John.

Johnny referred to Dulcie Zaccheus, a wonderful woman from India and extraordinary Christian prayer warrior, who had ministered to him in his hour of need. Dulcie was small but mighty, no taller than five feet, with sparkling brown eyes and an absolutely serene demeanor. She was a rock of unbreakable faith. Dulcie had also made a great impression on Waylon—not enough for him to accept the Lord but enough for him to recognize the sincerity of her spiritual passion.

When it came to Waylon's salvation, I had to remember that old adage—just when you think you've been patient enough is when you require even more patience. I had, in fact, been patient in allowing Waylon to achieve sobriety in his way, not mine. But now that he was sober, my heart cried for him to open his eyes to the glory of God. Now that he was no longer high on mind-bending drugs, no longer hyper and unhinged, no longer going days without sleep, wouldn't Waylon's newfound clarity lead him directly to the loving bosom of Christ?

The answer, in short, was no. Not now. Not yet. I could force the issue—and I wanted to do just that. I could force-feed him Scripture and claim that it was prayer—my prayers and the prayers of others—that saw him through. I could read him the spiritual riot act. I could evangelize and proselytize till I turned blue in the face. I could do all this in the name of a loving God, but in the end, it wouldn't be a loving act. It would be an act born out of my own impatience, an act to assert my own insistence, my own ego, my own demand that Waylon receive Jesus according to my intractable plan.

With all that in mind, I decided to forgo planning Waylon's miraculous conversion and instead do something well within my limited capacity: plan another party.

Not that parties don't have a spiritual dimension. I believe they do. Parties—at least the ones I like to plan—can galvanize a community in the name of friendship. A good party can make meaningful connections and foster loving fellowship. Parties are also an opportunity to express creativity. I find it more meaningful when the party is organized around a creative theme. And when it came to creativity, the ambitious event I organized in December 1984 was a rousing success. I called it a Discovery Party.

The idea was to turn Southern Comfort into a showcase for clothing designers, illustrators, fine artists, and sculptors, who—in my opinion—deserved wider recognition. They deserved to be discovered. The unifying theme was the American West. I've long loved seeing images of the West—the landscape of my childhood—integrated in designs of all kinds. As a string quartet from Vanderbilt's Blair School of Music played chamber music, dozens of guests roamed through our house over the course of two days. I told Waylon that he could escape if he wanted to—his presence wasn't mandatory—but was delighted when, along with the other guests, he wandered from room to room to enjoy the various artistic impressions of the American West.

Waylon liked the spotlight. Most entertainers do. But he was also extremely generous in allowing the spotlight to fall on someone besides himself. Such was the case when I suggested we give a party to honor Chet Atkins.

"Beautiful idea," said Waylon. "Let's make it a really special night."

My motivation was to let Chet know that we both cherished him. In the wake of the Outlaw movement, the press had labeled Chet a super-conservative, a company man who'd roped in the renegades trying to break free.

Chet had been one of my earliest champions—the A&R executive who got my songs covered by Dottie West, Hank Locklin, and Don Gibson. He encouraged me to change my name. Chet was also the man who, on Bobby Bare's recommendation, brought Waylon to Nashville and signed him to RCA. Sure, Chet fretted about the drug habits of Waylon, Roger Miller, and Don Gibson. He told them—and rightfully so—that they were injuring themselves and the music. And sure, there were legitimate artistic differences between Chet and his artists. But at no time did anyone who worked with Chet disrespect his prowess as a producer or his virtuosity as a musician.

With all this in mind, Roger Miller and Don Gibson were the first guests I invited to a small dinner party for Chet and his witty wife, Leona.

The guests of honor were first to arrive.

"Chet's so magical," I told Leona in private. "Every time I've recorded with him it's been a thrill."

"You want him?" asked Leona. "You can have him."

In her quiet way, Leona had a wickedly wry sense of humor.

I wish I'd captured the evening on video. Highlights included Roger telling Don how he stole "Don Gibson licks" in writing "Lock, Stock and Teardrops," followed by Waylon's riveting rendition of the song; Roger singing Don's "Sweet Dreams" and "Old Lonesome Me"; Mark Knopfler of Dire Straits—a group Chet was currently recording—singing exquisite songs of his own; and finally, Don rendering a chillingly soulful version of his immortal "I Can't Stop Loving You."

It was an evening of hearty laughter, haunting music, and, most important, great healing. Each of us, in our own way, was able to express our gratitude to Chet Atkins and let him know that we dearly loved him.

Ironically, the party for Chet came not long after Waylon left the label—RCA—that Chet had led for so many years. It was without hard feelings or regrets that Waylon switched to MCA where he had good rapport with producer Jimmy Bowen, a fellow Texan, described by my husband as a man who approached country music with a "sense of sharp-creased style." Jimmy had been working at "Hillbilly Central"— Waylon's handle for Glaser Sound Studios—where he'd produced everyone from Mel Tillis to Hank Jr.

He and Waylon did two fascinating albums together—*Will the Wolf Survive?* and *Hangin' Tough*. In Waylon's judgment, though, neither record captured his newly sober soul. He thought he sounded rough and a little uncertain. He didn't like the timbre of his voice. The truth is that when Waylon quit drugs, he didn't quit cigarettes. In fact, his smoking increased and took a serious toll on his singing voice. It would take Waylon a while to find his footing as someone no longer dependent on chemical stimulants.

This transition period wasn't easy. Waylon worried that he'd lost his magical touch. Of course he hadn't. Every day I reassured him. And, for comfort, he'd ask me to go to the piano and sing a song I'd written for him years before, the same song that, when high as a kite, George Jones would insist I sing for him.

> I will dry the tears I see in your eyes
> And I feel the pain that you bring
> If ever your heart should live free and wild
> Darlin', darlin', it's yours
> Don't get me wrong, I'm not looking for pain
> But I must watch the sun set on you
> If ever your heart should walk in the night
> Darlin', darlin', it's yours

After I sang the song, he'd ask me to come sit close to him on the couch. He didn't have to say what was on his mind. I knew. He worried whether it was drugs that had boosted his creativity. I didn't share that worry. I knew that the source of creativity was far deeper than some man-made stimulant. I resisted the always-present temptation to preach, so instead simply said, "It's a gift you were given that can never be taken away."

"Are you sure?" he asked, with the innocence of a child.

"As sure as I love you—and that's as sure as sure can be."

The one present Waylon gave himself for giving up drugs required my participation. It happened during a winter trip to Arizona. Waylon had told me the backstory. As a kid in Littlefield, he had seen Jaybird Johnson, the local bootlegger, waltz into the local car dealer and pull three thousand dollars from his girlfriend's bra to buy a Cadillac.

"I promised myself," said Waylon, "that one day I was gonna do the same darn thing. Well, baby, that day is here."

So sure enough, we marched into the Caddie dealer in Phoenix where Waylon spotted a gold Seville with a customized stretched-out body. The salesman said there were only five like it in all the world.

Waylon nodded his head, waited a beat, and then said, "I'll take it."

The salesman was all smiles. But as he began directing us to his office to start the paperwork, Waylon stopped him.

"No need for a bunch of paperwork. Gonna pay cash."

And just like that, he reached into my bra where he'd stuffed a stash of bills that he handed to the wide-eyed salesman.

I was embarrassed to the core and turned every possible shade of red. The embarrassment deepened when Waylon saw fit to playfully pinch my butt.

But why not—I thought to myself—*who am I to get in the way of his boyhood fantasy?*

Embarrassed or not, I was happy for my man.

My happiness grew when I witnessed another gift of sobriety— Waylon taking command of his organization. In the haze of the drug days, he had neglected the business side. His accountant-manager Neil

Reshen, for example, had been given free rein. Upon closer scrutiny, Waylon discovered that not all Neil's dealings were on the up-and-up and the man had to be let go. Then there was the unacceptable behavior of some of his band members who were acting as though, in their supporting role, their stardom was as great as Waylon's. Like Neil, they'd been getting away with a lot. Waylon put a stop to all this and assumed a strong leadership role. Finally, he had the clarity to assume full responsibility for every aspect of his professional life. At long last he was in charge.

Chapter 25

UNEXPECTED BIRTH

JOHNNY CASH HAD INVITED WAYLON, WILLIE, AND KRIS Kristofferson to appear on his annual Christmas television program. This particular year—1984—he decided to tape the show in Montreux, Switzerland. At the press conference to promote the show, a reporter asked the four assembled stars, "Why Montreux?"

Waylon was quick with a quip.

"Because this is where the baby Jesus was born," he said.

As they went on to tape the show, I felt a strange sensation, there in the magnificent setting of the snowcapped Swiss Alps, that although these four men were the most rugged of rugged individualists, they fit together in a way that one seemed to complete another. Or, as Waylon put it, "This funny-looking quartet was born, again like the baby Jesus, out of an immaculate conception."

The concept itself probably sprang from Chips Moman's fertile musical mind. Johnny had hired Chips as his soundman in Montreux. Back in Nashville, Chips was also producing tracks on Willie and John when Kris and Waylon happened to visit the studio. That's when Chips mentioned a tune called "The Highwayman" that he had taught them back in Switzerland. All four guys liked the song.

"So let's cut it," Chips said.

Amazingly, not one of these nonconformists chose to noncon-form. They were happy to go along for the ride.

As it turned out, "The Highwayman," an epic composition by Jimmy Webb, struck a powerful chord in each of the four artists. The song was high drama and deep mythology. Waylon played the part of a dam builder, Kris a sailor, Johnny a starship commander, and Willie the highwayman himself.

I was in the studio with the guys when, after the final take, Chips announced, "It's a smash!"

Chips was right. The single, "The Highwayman," a number-one hit, soon morphed into the supergroup, the Highwaymen. On their first album, the poignant "Desperados Waiting for a Train," written by Guy Clark, also registered as a hit.

Seeing it as a boost for everyone's career, Mark Rothbaum, Willie's super-sharp manager, booked a few dates for the quartet that sold out immediately. Then the idea further flowered into a full tour.

At first Kris was skeptical. He didn't think the four men, no matter how great their mutual respect, could pull it together. Kris didn't want to desert his band. Johnny had scheduling conflicts. Willie had his picnics to worry about. But because of Waylon's determination to pull everyone together, it came off.

Each artist was told he could take one or two of his own band members on the tour. The scheduling puzzles were solved and some-how the problems disappeared with almost supernatural aplomb.

In Waylon's autobiography, he gave his impression of the camara-derie that characterized the group:

Me and Kris think John and Willie are like Truman and MacArthur. They won't admit it, but there's a little competition between them. Willie might be late getting to the stage, and John will say, "Where's

Willie? I'm going back to my dressing room." Both of them enjoy their star power. When John went to the Eastern bloc countries, they called him "Your Majesty," and he liked that, until he found out it was a guy from the KGB.

[John] looks like he comes from a different historical era. He could've been Jesse James, or the Apostle Paul . . . who said, "Woe be unto me if I don't preach the gospel." . . . If he's Paul, Willie must be Saint Peter. He floats freely, founding his church on whatever rock he cares to perch on. . . . Kris taught us how to write great poetry. . . . He's probably the only truly theatrical performer among us, a true actor in every sense of the word. Kris is probably the most enthusiastic about the music.[1]

As a grand scheme, the Highwaymen turned into a decade-long project—from 1985 through 1995—with three separate albums and several grueling but exciting tours that spanned the globe. At every stage, it turned into a beautiful musical phenomenon that I was privileged to witness. It even led to the four heroes being cast into a movie, a remake of the 1939 western classic *Stagecoach* that was shot in Phoenix in 1986, in which I had a small role opposite Tony Franciosa.

The process itself was tedious, the script was lame, and the high point came when Lash LaRue, who had a cameo in the film, dropped by our bus. When Johnny got word, he rushed over. As young boys, Waylon and Johnny had idolized this movie cowboy, famous for his bullwhip. Now sitting across from Lash, Waylon and Johnny turned into twelve-year-olds. They were practically giddy. Waylon talked about every one of Lash's films—from *Son of Billy the Kid* to *Mark of the Lamb*. He also told the story of when LaRue had come to the Palace, the movie theater in Littlefield, Texas. During his stage act, Lash had inadvertently ripped the big screen with his whip. Enraged, the theater owner said, "You're going to pay for this!" And Lash said,

"I've got a gun and a whip that says I won't."

LaRue smiled and said he remembered that incident.

"Man," said Waylon, "your attitude that night was something I'll never forget. I do believe it changed my life."

The Highwaymen enterprise certainly changed our lives, and all for the good. In the best sense, it was a family affair. Of the family memories, the strongest I have are of Lisa Kristofferson, one of the world's great women, managing her five children during the day while Kris, exhausted from the previous night's show, slept in. With one child on her hip, another on her breast, and the others in tow behind her, Lisa would intrepidly lead our treks to the zoo, museum, or amusement park. I had Shooter, and Annie Nelson—Willie's fourth wife—had her sons Micah and Lukas. We all loved being in one another's company. The kids had a blast. We forged friendships that would last a lifetime. But it was Lisa and her formidable brand of motherhood that inspired me most.

On off-days, June and Johnny went shopping. An industrious spirit, June would bargain hunt whenever she could, amassing huge trunks of clothing and knickknacks that she'd ship to their home in Hendersonville and later sell at a profit. Willie was always looking for a golf game, occasionally recruiting Kris. Waylon would usually hang out with Shooter and me, exploring the exotic tourist spots in Sydney or Singapore.

Before the shows I caught glimpses of what I saw as little-boy rivalries. Johnny would pop his head into Waylon's dressing room, look around, and say, "Just wanna make sure they didn't give you anything that they didn't give me." But once onstage, the musical mood was always majestic. From where I stood in the wings, I envisioned their profiles on Mount Rushmore. Four titans. At the same time, they were also four little boys who'd just happened to have grown tall and wore boots.

Their passion was their music. I never tired of hearing "Mystery Train" or "Folsom Prison Blues" or "Blue Eyes Crying in the Rain" or "Me and Bobby McGee" or "Amanda" or "Good Hearted Woman" or "Mammas, Don't Let Your Babies Grow Up to Be Cowboys" or "Sunday Morning Coming Down" or "Are You Sure Hank Done It This Way" or "A Boy Named Sue" or "Always on My Mind." The songs were always the same and yet the songs were always different—different interpretations, vocal combinations, and harmonies. The spontaneity never lagged. The surprises never stopped.

The hallmark was humor. The guys thrived on it. Not a day passed without some funny incident. One of the funniest didn't start out funny. It began as we set off for Europe when Waylon suggested that Jack "Cowboy" Clement take charge of the sound system. Kris, John, and Willie agreed. I had my reservations. Beyond his musical prowess, Cowboy was a wild card, a man who might do or say anything. But because my role in this great enterprise was restricted to being a supportive and loving wife, I didn't say a word.

After the first show that Cowboy worked, he approached Willie.

"Your rhythm's off," said Cowboy. "You start in last week and wind up next week. You don't stay on the beat."

In no uncertain terms, Willie told Cowboy where to go and what to do.

But Cowboy was undeterred. After the next show he stayed on Willie, telling him that he was singing "Good Hearted Woman" twice as fast as it should be sung.

Willie heard enough. He told Waylon that he wanted Cowboy fired. That would leave the Highwaymen in the middle of Europe without a soundman.

Kris came by to see Waylon after the incident.

"Where are you going?" asked Waylon.

"To smoke a joint with Willie."

"Maybe you should smoke two. And when you get halfway down the second joint, gently suggest to Willie that he might have been a little hasty with Cowboy."

Kris took the suggestion. A half hour later he and Willie walked—or floated—out of Willie's dressing room.

With smiling eyes, Willie came up to Waylon and said, "Cowboy probably didn't mean no harm. Let's give the man a second chance."

A major victory for marijuana diplomacy.

Waylon was forced to seek another kind of diplomacy when, in the course of one of the tours, he learned that the merchandising company's promise to pay each of the four artists a $25,000 advance was being reneged.

Waylon was obligated to bring this unfortunate update to Kris, John, and Willie, who had congregated on Willie's bus. The challenge, though, was a rule that positive-thinking Willie strictly enforced: no negative news was allowed on his bus.

Waylon, who greatly respected Willie's mandate, paused before climbing on the bus. How to break the bad news without breaking Willie's rule?

When Waylon finally walked on the bus and faced his colleagues, he was ready. He said, "Okay, guys, how many of you are still expecting an advance from the merchandise firm of twenty-five grand?"

As Willie began to raise his hand, Waylon quickly blurted out, "Not so fast, Willie."

Their bond, of course, overwhelmed their differences. Waylon always talked about their shared commitment to music, their ability, as he put it, "to blend the early country of the Carter family with Texas swing, southern gospel, and rockabilly."

They also shared a common sense of destiny. "There's not one of us," said Waylon, "who hasn't come face-to-face with his own mortality, and many's the time we've gone through our struggles and survivals together."

The decade-long life of the Highwaymen was a marvel. To watch these four troubadours, grizzled and world-weary, grow even closer in spirit was a unique blessing.

"It wasn't that we put aside our egos," Waylon said. "Each of us has too much ego to ever do that. But somehow our egos blended. Somehow our egos—ornery as they were—learned to harmonize."

Chapter 26

HOSS

I REMEMBER A REPORTER ASKING ME ABOUT MY OWN EGO. IT was 1987 and the interview, at Southern Comfort, came in the aftermath of Waylon's *A Man Called Hoss*, a dazzling autobiographical concept album.

I was raving about Waylon's endlessly creative energy and how, in ten songs, he had so succinctly summed up the essence of his life.

"But what about your songs?" the reporter asked me. "What about your energy? It's been six years since your last album, *Ridin' Shotgun*."

"Actually only three years since I recorded *Rock and Roll Lullaby*," I said. He didn't know about my album that had disappeared right after Chips Moman's label went belly up. I told him the story and he, an enthusiastic Jessi Colter fan, was delighted when I gave him one of the few remaining copies.

"Can't wait to listen to it," he said, "but I'm guessing it must be frustrating to record an album that never gets heard."

"Sure it is," I confessed.

"And I'm wondering if it's equally frustrating for a talented singer-songwriter like you to . . . well, to live in the shadow of your husband.

We all have egos, and I'm curious how being in the background affects yours?"

"Have you listened carefully to *A Man Called Hoss*?" I asked.

"I know it's about Waylon's life."

"He wrote a song about me that might answer your question better than I can."

I got up, put the album on the turntable and placed the needle on a song Waylon called "Jessi: You Deserve the Stars in My Crown."

> You're the one who took the time
> Looked for a reason to believe
> You finally found a sun
> Which shines on the better side of me
>
> More than anyone
> You're a part of all I say and do
> When it's all said and done
> When they remember me, they'll think of you
>
> You always believed
> That's what brought me up when I was down
> And I do believe
> You deserve the stars in my crown

Moved by the song, the reporter asked, "So you're saying you're happy being a supporter?"

"It's more than support," I said. "It's love."

"So you're happy to put your career on the back burner?"

"Look, my career happened almost in spite of myself. I've always loved singing, and I've always loved writing. And I'm certain that I'll always do both. But formulating or forging a career, spending time planning and plotting about how to raise my public profile—that's just not me."

"Yet it does seem to be Waylon."

"And justifiably so," I said. "Waylon's a creative genius. I'm not. I don't say that to denigrate my talent. I thank God for my talent. I consider talent a precious commodity. I try to cultivate and grow my talent as best I can. But there's a difference between abundant talent and outrageous genius. Waylon thinks, sleeps, dreams, and breathes musical constructs. He never stops creating, not for a second. He hears, feels, and sees things most people don't. And he's unable to rest until he expresses those things in musical form. His restless spirit is always at work. The result of that work is a gift for everyone, me included. I want to encourage that work, even as he has always encouraged my work."

"So you will get back to recording."

"You bet."

"Anytime soon?"

"I have no timetable. I have a young son to look after. I have a daughter who's become a fine young woman. I have a husband who deserves my attention. And, above all, I have a relationship with God that sustains my spirit."

Waylon's sober spirit was growing stronger every day. The release of *A Man Called Hoss* confirmed his ability to create abundantly without drug-induced energy. He wrote hauntingly self-reflective songs about his childhood ("Littlefield" and "You'll Never Take the Texas Out of Me"), his old loves ("A Love Song I Can't Sing Anymore"), his relationship with Nashville ("If Ole Hank Could Only See Us Now"), his brutal battles with cocaine ("Rough and Rowdy Days"), and, finally, his victory over drugs ("I'm Living Proof There's Life After You").

"This is an incredible record," I told Waylon. "This is the best work you've done in years."

"Couldn't have done it high," said Waylon. "I see that now. For years I was convinced that I needed that bump to get past the creative block. Now I know that jumping over that block ain't the way. I had to walk through that block. I had to walk through that fear. 'Cause on the other side I found a clarity I never knew was there. Clarity's the key. When I was whacked out of my mind, I thought I was as clear as a bell. But looking back, I see that I confused chaos for clarity."

With the chaos behind us, I thanked God for our new life, anchored in a steady calmness.

It wasn't that Waylon had lost any of his spontaneity and irrepressible energy—Waylon was still Waylon—but the manic behavior, the crazy binges, and the periodic disappearances were now things of the past. His demons, finally defeated, were no longer on the attack.

An attack, however, did come in another frightening form.

In early 1988, we were playing the Crazy Horse, a huge venue in Orange County, California. Back in the dressing room between shows, Waylon lit a cigarette and found it difficult to inhale.

Seeing the pained look on his face, I asked, "What's wrong?"

"A pain."

"Where?"

"My chest."

"Just stay where you are," I said. "I'll be back with help."

The closest to a doctor I could find was a paramedic working as a bouncer. He knew right away that Waylon was having a heart attack.

Assuming his macho-man role, Waylon said, "It's not that bad. Besides, I got another show to do."

I enlisted the support of Fred Reiser, the owner of the Crazy Horse, who told Waylon, "Don't even think about doing another show."

The pain must have been excruciating because Waylon agreed to immediately go to a nearby clinic where the attending doctor looked just like Larry Gatlin, the one country singer my husband never liked.

"Bad omen," said Waylon.

"Good omen," I said, when the doctor advised an injection of TPA—tissue plasminogen activator—that breaks down blood clots. Waylon took the physician's advice. The wonder drug did its job. When we learned that single dose cost eight thousand dollars, Waylon said, "If I'd been poor, I'd been dead."

Waylon rested in his room while I went back to our hotel to get some of his things. On the return trip to the clinic, I saw that police cars and media trucks had surrounded the place. My initial thought was that Waylon had died. Imagine my relief when I found him resting comfortably in his room. It turned out that while I was away a Hell's Angel had broken into the place and shot a patient on the operating table.

Before leaving the clinic, Waylon underwent an angioplasty, another attempt to fully open his blocked arteries, that was only partially successful. Convinced he had the problem licked, Waylon went back on the road. But a few months later, on his way to play a Johnny Cash benefit in Bristol, Tennessee, he experienced severe pain and turned the bus around.

"You didn't have a heart attack," the doctor said, "but you're about to. Those clogged arteries are a ticking time bomb. You need a bypass, and you need it now."

As it turned out, Waylon needed a quadruple bypass. The next day I checked him in to Nashville's Baptist Hospital. His first pre-op visitor was Johnny Cash.

"Hey, hoss," said Johnny. "Just dropped by to make sure you get through this thing okay."

"Thanks, John," said Waylon, "but to tell you the truth, you don't look too good yourself. You're ashen."

"Strange that you say that, 'cause I am feeling a little weak."

"Why don't you have one of the docs check you out," Waylon suggested.

Next thing we knew, Johnny was in a hospital gown in the room next to Waylon's with June by his side. Tests indicated severe artery blockage. He, too, required a bypass.

Despite the severity of the situation, the jokes started flying. Although the men were no more than a few feet apart, the doctors didn't want them out of bed, so they kept calling each other on the phone.

"How's it going in there?" asked Johnny.

"Lousy," said Waylon.

"Why?"

"I'm hurting like the dickens, but it turns out I'm allergic to morphine."

"Feel sorry for you, buddy," said Johnny, "'cause I ain't allergic to nothing. They're pouring that morphine into me and, believe me, I'm feeling no pain."

"That's what I get for saving your life. You get high while I suffer."

"Suffering is noble," Johnny stated. "The more you suffer, the greater your character."

"I'd like to trade in some of that greatness for a little of your morphine."

The other point of contention had to do with the press. Johnny and June were calling press conferences to talk about his condition. The last thing in the world Waylon wanted were reporters nosing around his room.

"Can't we keep this low key?" asked Waylon.

"No, sir. If we both kick the bucket, I wanna make sure I get the headline, not you," said Johnny.

Naturally that made Waylon laugh, though laughing hurt.

Thank God both operations were successful.

Johnny and Waylon had to remain in the hospital, of course, for post-op care—which was when the kidding reconvened.

"I measure my strength," Waylon told Johnny, "by my ability to reach out when Jessi walks by my bed and pinch her on the butt. For the past three days, I haven't been able to do it. But this morning, by God, I caught her."

"So you're back to feeling like a superstar," said Johnny.

"After this experience, I'm not sure I'll ever feel like a star again."

"What makes you say that, hoss?"

"When these nurses get me up to walk the hallway, I can hardly stand. But they get me up anyway. They put me in one of those gowns. They take my arms and get me going, and there I am, halfway down the hallway, when I feel a draft from behind. That's when I realize this gown ain't got no back, and I got no shorts on, and folks are looking at my bare behind. That's the great equalizer."

Another topic of conversation became how and when they would each exit the hospital. Johnny preferred to do it with fanfare. Waylon wanted to leave quietly.

"We'll compromise," said John. "We'll leave together."

"Agreed."

And when they did, the press was waiting, both men standing before the cameras, arm in arm.

For now, Waylon's sickness had been abated. Modern medicine had given him—and Johnny—a life extension. But sickness would manifest in other forms. For all Waylon's determination to lead a robust and productive life, for all the strength of his undiminished spirit, his stamina was permanently compromised. Physically, he would never be the same again.

Part Five

THE ROAD BACK HOME

Chapter 27

NOURISHMENT

Early in our relationship, Waylon told me his name means "land by the highway."

"I may settle on that land for a short spell," he said, "but the highway is always calling. And, to be truthful, I can't see myself ignoring that call."

One of Waylon's favorite expressions was "The bus rolls at midnight." Such a large chunk of our lives was lived on the road where the culinary code was "Eat what you can, when you can—and gobble it down fast."

Some of our earliest clashes were about food. Waylon was always hungry and I was always tired of cooking. I realized, though, that part of my job would involve kitchen duties—and I reluctantly accepted the role. I was head-over-heels in love with a man who both fascinated and frightened me. I never got over the fascination but I did get over the fright. He was, after all, just a man in search of love.

Giving love meant giving nourishment. But my Arizona style of cooking one-dish meals wouldn't cut it. Waylon didn't like casseroles or sauces. Waylon liked everything fried, cooked separately, and well done. He loved white bread and white sugar. He devoured huge quantities of cheese, eggs, sausages, gravy, and buttermilk biscuits swabbed with jelly. For a midnight snack, he'd refry a dozen doughnuts in butter. After he gave up drugs, he went from smoking two or three packs of cigarettes to six or seven.

The bypass operation changed all that, setting off an alarm he could no longer ignore.

He stopped smoking—cold turkey—and, for the first time in his life, he pursued what Maureen, our assistant, and I had been advocating for years: a healthy low-fat diet.

It wasn't easy. Waylon was a man of enormous appetite in all areas of life. He loved the comfort food that had emotionally sustained him since childhood. He realized the urgent necessity of eliminating the vast majority of those items from his menu, but that didn't make it easy. He suffered withdrawal from nicotine. He hungered for those sugary substances and deep-fried delicacies he'd always found so satisfying.

I give him great credit for changing his ways. His willpower was astounding. He wanted to live. He wanted to prolong this new chapter of his life when, finally free of drugs, he could settle back and with hard-earned calmness enjoy his music and, even more significantly, relish his role as husband and dad.

In 1989, the year after the bypass, Waylon turned fifty-two and Shooter turned ten. Shooter was crazy for toys. He and Waylon would spend hours with the Ninja warriors. They loved going to toy stores together to check out the latest exotic imports from Japan. When Shooter reached his teen years, he became a computer prodigy before becoming a musical prodigy and ultimately merging the two. Not only did he draw his dad into his complex computer games, he also began introducing Waylon to heavy metal and alternative rock. It was Shooter, who greatly admired Trent Reznor and Nine Inch Nails, who broadened his dad's musical outlook.

"My father really didn't have prejudices when it came to music," Shooter told me. "He just lacked exposure. At heart, Dad was a raw rock and roller. When he heard the real thing, he responded positively. He felt camaraderie with some of the most far-out bands of the day because he himself was far out.

"As I explored new styles of music that most men Dad's age considered outrageous, he wasn't outraged at all. He liked how I went places he hadn't ever gone, and he was happy to follow me there. I have a funny story about the time he followed me to the mall. In a move of solidarity, he decided to get his ear pierced. But rather than have me take him to some weird piercing parlor, we went to Claire's, a store that sold costume jewelry to teenyboppers, where a sweet seventeen-year-old girl pierced his ear. Dad was glad that she had no idea who he was."

In 1990, the Highwaymen reunited for their second album, continuing with Chips Moman as producer. I was especially touched by the song Waylon wrote with Roger Murrah for the project, "Angels Love Bad Men." He called it a reflection of his past.

When his stolen gold has turned to rust
He rides off in a cloud of dust
Lookin' for a border he can cross
She'll stand by and watch him go
Wonderin' if he'll ever know
The hurt she's feelin' now, and what they've lost

Angels love bad men, that's how it's always been
They give their whole hearts when they fall
Angels love bad men, that's how it's always been
Love holds their hearts against the wall

When his corporate day comes to an end
He rides away in his Mercedes Benz
Soon he's lost beneath the neon sky
Outside of town, in their suburban home
She spends another night alone
And wonders what went wrong, wonders why

Listening to the song, I wondered about Waylon's ongoing resistance to the acceptance of Christ in his life. I wondered whether he still viewed himself as a "bad man," someone incapable of self-forgiveness or the forgiveness of God Almighty. It was a tricky question because, as I had learned long ago, even in the mildest form, proselytizing would never work with Waylon.

At the same time, I knew that Waylon's interest in spirituality had certainly grown. The best evidence was his relationship with minister Will Campbell. Brother Will was going through a rough financial patch and needed a job. Waylon and I loved the man. We'd both read *Dragon to a Butterfly*, his riveting autobiography, praised by everyone from President Jimmy Carter to writers Walker Percy and Robert Penn Warren. Waylon especially admired how, in President Carter's words, Brother Will "tore down the walls that separated white and black Southerners."

"If you want work," Waylon told him, "come over to the house tonight. The bus rolls at midnight."

Will came out on the road with us for several trips. His job was undefined. If anyone asked me, I said he was Waylon's spiritual advisor. Waylon simply liked having the man around.

During one long trek, I heard Will ask Waylon, "Hey, man, what do you believe?"

Waylon hesitated before answering. When he did speak, all he said was, "Yeah."

Will lived with the answer for a few minutes before saying, "'Yeah'? What's that supposed to mean?"

"Yeah means yeah," was Waylon's only response. The conversation ended there.

Brother Will was cool. He knew not to probe further. He understood the mandate of Saint Francis who said, "Preach the gospel at all times; when necessary, use words." In addressing the issue of Waylon's soul, words were not necessary. The mere fact that he wanted a blood-washed believer like Will Campbell in his presence was evidence that God was stirring his heart.

It wasn't long after that Waylon started working on "I Do Believe," a song recorded by the Highwaymen on their third and final album, *The Road Goes On Forever*, produced by Don Was.

After writing it, Waylon sang the song for me, and then for Brother Will.

"What do you think?" asked Waylon.

"That'll preach," answered Will.

The song said:

> In my own way I'm a believer
> In my own way right or wrong
> I don't talk too much about it
> It's something I keep working on
> I don't have too much to build on
> My faith has never been that strong
>
> There is a man in that old building
> He's a holy man, they say
> He keeps talking about tomorrow
> While I keep struggling with today
> He preaches hellfire and brimstone
> And heaven seems so far away
>
> I do believe in a higher power
> One that loves us one and all
> Not someone to solve our problems
> Or to catch me when I fall
> He gave us all a mind to think with
> And to know what's right or wrong
> He is that inner spirit
> That keeps us strong

In my own way I'm a believer
But not in voices I can't hear
I believe in a loving father
One I never have to fear
That I should live life at its fullest
Just as long as I am here

I love the song's honesty, especially Waylon's confession that he hasn't "too much to build on" because his faith "has never been that strong." Of course he's talking about his experience with his childhood church, the same church that, in the second verse, is led by "a holy man" preaching the gospel of fear. In the face of that negative indoctrination, the song is a straight-up declaration of faith. For the first time ever, Waylon defined himself as a believer. He avoided the word *God* but not the term *higher power*. I was deeply moved that he called that higher power—that "inner spirit"—"a loving father."

The song thrilled me to my core. I viewed it as unequivocal acceptance of a loving Creator.

"But why not call that Creator by name?" I asked.

"You want me to call him Jesus?" asked Waylon.

"He *is* Jesus."

"Why is the name so important to you, Jessi? What's in a name?"

"Truth is in his name. Love is in his name. Forgiveness is in his name. Mercy is in his name. Everything is in his name—all the infinite glory of his redemptive story."

"You're preaching," Waylon said with a smile.

"Didn't Brother Will say you were preaching in that song? When we believe something with all our heart, we want the world to know."

"I'm not telling the world to believe what I believe, Jessi. I'm just saying that I do believe."

"But in what?"

"In love—and the spirit of love. Isn't that enough?"

I paused for a second. I took a deep breath. I realized this discussion was taking the wrong turn. I saw that once again impatience was marring my outlook.

"You know what," I said, "love is enough. Your song is beautiful, the way you express your feelings is beautiful. You're beautiful, Waylon, and I love you."

His megawatt wider-than-Texas smile said it all.

Chapter 28

WILL THE CIRCLE
BE UNBROKEN?

IN 1994, WAYLON AND I WERE SET TO CELEBRATE OUR twenty-fifth wedding anniversary. Twenty-five years. Hard to believe. Hard to conceive of the joy I felt, knowing our bond was stronger than ever. Hard to imagine how swiftly the years had flown by. Hard to process the extreme vicissitudes we had both experienced. Hard to contain the gratitude I felt for the love and excitement this man had brought into my life.

Our plan was to celebrate at Big Cedar, a lush wilderness resort outside of Branson, Missouri. Waylon liked my suggestion that we invite the entire extended family—all our children and their loved ones. It was a big brood, and it had been years since we'd all been together.

There was boating, fishing, horseback riding, and hikes in the woods. In the evenings we met up at the lodge and sang songs in front of a crackling fireplace. It was a beautiful gathering.

On the third day we were there, Waylon and I were at lunch on the veranda overlooking the woodsy landscape when he said, "I had a strange dream last night."

"Tell me about it, dear."

"It was a nightmare. I asked you to marry me and you said no."

"That is strange. I'd never say no."

"What if I asked you now?"

"You don't have to. If memory serves me right, it was twenty-five years ago when I said yes."

"But if you hadn't said yes then, would you say yes now?"

"Of course," I said. "A million times over."

"Then say it. Say you'll marry me."

"What is this about?"

"I'm proposing."

"Again?"

"Yes, again. Jessi Colter, will you marry me?"

"Of course."

"Then say it."

"I will. I do."

"Great. Now go up to our room where your gown will be waiting for you."

Behind my back, Waylon had it all planned out. In an elaborate ceremony, presided over by surprise guest minister Will Campbell, we were to be married that night.

Our irreplaceable assistant Maureen, who knew me as well as anyone, had ordered the dress from Neiman Marcus. Complete with veil and long train, the gown was gorgeous: designed in white satin, bejeweled with tiny pearls, and accented with delicate lace. I was breathless.

Looking especially dashing in his custom-tailored tuxedo, Waylon escorted me to a horse-drawn carriage covered in white lilies and roses. We rode in style to an extravagantly decorated cabin where our family was waiting.

Brother Will spoke words that warmed my heart. He spoke of the sanctity of our marriage in the name of the living God. Waylon didn't wince. He accepted those words without reservation.

"This is the woman who has changed my life," he told those who had come to witness the ceremony. "This is the woman who has saved my life. And this is the woman who, with the patience of Job, has put up with more than any of us can imagine."

Everyone chuckled, but I was too teary-eyed to laugh.

All I could say was, "This is the man who completes me. This is the man whose goodness radiates from the very depths of his soul."

That night, alone in our room, Waylon held me in his arms.

"Happy?" he asked.

"Overjoyed."

The joy that characterized the earlier Highwaymen tours began to dissipate during the final shows supporting *The Road Goes On Forever*. The domestic concerts were fine, but by the time we reached Thailand, which was in the throes of an AIDS epidemic, Waylon was bone-tired. He also began experiencing respiratory problems, exacerbated by the stifling pollution in Hong Kong and Singapore.

When we arrived home, Waylon required a couple of weeks to regain his strength. Although his stamina was compromised, his creative juices kept flowing.

In spite of his failing health, Waylon produced some of his best music—albums like *The Eagle* and the hilariously titled *Too Dumb for New York City, Too Ugly for L.A.* Reflecting on his past, he turned out the wonderful *Ol' Waylon Sings Ol' Hank*, *Waymore's Blues*, *Right for the Time*, and *Closing In on the Fire*. Creatively, the fire burned brightly.

His bond with Shooter also expanded his horizons, renewed his interest in fatherhood, and got him to thinking more about young people. We helped each other out on two separate albums we did for children—Waylon's was *Cowboys, Sisters, Rascals and Dirt*; mine was *Jessi Colter Sings Just for Kids: Songs from Around the World*.

A reporter came to profile me in the aftermath of my kids record. I remember that her first question startled me.

"Where have you been?" she asked.

I took a second to gather my thoughts before answering, "Right here in Nashville."

"But you haven't been releasing records."

"Well, I'm releasing this one now. It's for children of all races and religions."

"I've heard it, I like it, but I also have to ask you about having sacrificed your career."

I smiled and said, "I haven't sacrificed a thing. I feel incredibly blessed. I have a beautiful life."

"With all due respect, I know Waylon is one of the greats. But if half of what they say about him is true, he must be a handful."

"He's a blessing," I assured her. "I look around and see nothing but blessings. And besides, if Waylon is a handful, so am I. We're all broken vessels, aren't we?"

"Do you have plans to make more records?"

"When the time is right, yes."

In 1998, the time was right for Waylon to get back together with our dear friend Shel Silverstein and collaborate on a lovely album they called *Old Dogs*. The old dogs themselves—the singers on the record—were Waylon, Bobby Bare, Mel Tillis, and Jerry Reed. Shel wrote the songs, all about aging, and the dogs sang them with the kind of sensitivity only seniority allows.

It turned out to be one of Waylon's last sessions and one of the most poignant of his career. And though his hunger to write, record, and perform never waned, his energy did. He grew increasingly tired. He'd been diagnosed as diabetic. Together with his history of heart disease, the inability to process blood sugar was taking a steady toll on his overall well-being. Those sleepless years of abusing his body had caught up with him.

By the end of the decade, Waylon, only in his early sixties, was having a hard time tolerating the cold Nashville winters.

"I'm feeling the need for warmth," he said. "I'm missing the way it feels to be in the desert when that midday sun shines all over my face."

"I'm always missing Arizona," I said.

"Wanna go back?" he asked.

"I'd love to. It's home."

"It's where I really got started. Where we met."

"The Valley of the Sun."

"Bring it on."

Chapter 29

THIS MORTAL COIL

I WAS THINKING OF THE BELOVED HELEN D. PERKINS JOHNSON
and an old hymn the saints would sing in her church:

> I was standing by my window
> On one cold and cloudy day
> When I saw that hearse come rolling
> For to carry my mother away
>
> Will the circle be unbroken
> By and by, Lord, by and by
> There's a better home a-waiting
> In the sky, Lord, in the sky[1]

It wasn't a cold and cloudy day in Paradise Valley. The sun was shining brilliantly, Waylon was napping peacefully in our bedroom, and I was seated in the den of our winter home that my dear brother Johnny had found for us overlooking the vast Arizona desert. I was drifting back into the landscape of my childhood, remembering the way Mother would artfully weave the tapestry of her sermons so that the stories were lifelike pictures for all to see: Jesus with the woman at the well; Jesus turning water to wine; Jesus calming the raging sea; Jesus healing the blind, feeding the five thousand, weeping in the garden.

Those stories still lived in my heart and informed my mind, bringing back memories of the woman who had shaped my spirit—and the spirits of countless others—with the words she spoke and the kindness she extended. I also thought of Daddy, his wondrous mine and lifelong pursuit of minerals hidden deep beneath the earth. My precious parents, long gone, weren't gone at all, especially here in the territory outside Phoenix where they had arrived, brave souls in search of a new life.

A new life was what Waylon was seeking—a new life inspired by a former life, a time when he had come to Arizona, a young man who'd been traumatized by the death of his mentor Buddy Holly and yet found success and even stardom, thanks to the wild enthusiasm of the college kids who'd frequented JD's outsized barroom.

"There was an energy back then," Waylon remembered, "that let me find myself. And let me be myself. I believe it was the mystical energy of the desert, that same energy I needed to kick drugs. So many good things that have happened to me happened in that desert, the best being meeting you. That desert, strange and mysterious as it is, has healing properties. Can't explain it."

"You don't have to," I said. "The healing has already started. I can feel it."

The healing, as it turned out, was not physical. It was spiritual.

As a result of diabetes, neuropathy set in, causing Waylon extreme pain all along his legs. Soon he was unable to drive.

I took over the wheel. From Waylon's point of view, that took some getting used to. As the daughter of a car builder, I'm a confident and relaxed driver. Waylon recognized that but he also couldn't resist backseat driving at virtually every turn. I understood. It was hard for him to give up that kind of control.

He often asked me to drive him to the old haunts, the places—like Coolidge, Arizona—where he had lived with his first wife and children. He wanted to see scenes of his past. In viewing those scenes, he'd speak of his regrets, his shortcomings as a young man.

"I did foolish things," he said. "I wound up hurting myself, but mainly I hurt other people. That's what hurts me the most now."

"God is forgiving," I said.

"God may be, but I'm not."

"That's the point of prayer. We pray to be like him. We pray to forgive ourselves just as he forgives us."

Forgiveness is a slow process, especially with a man like Waylon who felt as though anything he achieved had to be earned by the sweat of his brow.

There was so much I wanted to say, but I knew how words can get in the way. We'd drive into the desert at sunset and watch the world turn burnished gold. We'd simply sit there in silence, holding hands, breathing in the magnificent setting.

Finally Waylon would say, "You talk about grace. You say it's free. We can all have it. It's God's gift. Well, believing that is one thing, but feeling it—really feeling it in your heart and soul—man, that's another thing altogether."

"The feeling comes when it comes," I said.

"I'm impatient, Jessi. You know that. When I wanted to feel a certain way, I'd pop a pill. When I wanted to feel another way, I'd snort a line. Those were feelings I could control . . . until I couldn't. Until they controlled me. But good or bad, they were feelings I could count on. Feelings I understood. So I gotta ask you—how do you feel grace?"

"I know it isn't easy. It's like finding something that's already there. Long ago I found something Charlotte Brontë wrote in a novel I love, *Jane Eyre*. She wrote, 'I need not sell my soul to buy bliss. I have an inward treasure born with me which can keep me alive if all extraneous delights should be withheld or offered at a price I cannot afford to give.'"

"An inward treasure," Waylon repeated.

"It's there," I said. "We have to be still enough, quiet enough, faithful enough to find it."

"Or let it find us."

"Amen."

A new millennium arrived. Shooter, now twenty-one, left Nashville for Los Angeles to pursue a music career of his own. Waylon, who had lovingly guided him since infancy, knew that our son was well prepared. He gave his blessing. At the same time, he felt it was time to give up Southern Comfort and permanently move to Arizona. The desert kept calling.

We bought a comfortable house in Chandler with a calm ambience and enchanting views. Waylon's health worsened but his spirit stayed strong. I never saw fear in his eyes. I saw determination—not to live forever but to live each day fully. Loving people surrounded us. A neighbor, a former FBI hostage negotiator, became one of Waylon's best late-life buddies. They spent hours entertaining each other with stories of their wild adventures.

Jenny Lynn Hollowell, a wonderful cellist and a fiddler, was another great spirit who'd come by and play her enchanting music, filling the house with joy. Our faithful friend Maureen came from Nashville as well as Coach James Denver Burke. Maureen had met Coach when she taught at Tennessee Preparatory School. He ran their athletic program and took one of his teams, named after Waylon, to a state championship. Coach came to work with us as security but soon became one of Waylon's most trusted confidants. When we moved to Chandler, Coach was an essential member of our household staff.

That staff was small. Waylon did not want to be around strangers, only friends. He didn't want pity or even sympathy, only love. Some of the strongest love came from Dulcie Zaccheus, the woman whose Wayside Ministry we had supported for years. Waylon greatly respected and recognized her for what she was: the living spirit of

Christ Jesus. Calling from California, Dulcie would speak to Waylon at great length, although she knew he was still not ready to utter the words I yearned to hear.

Waylon grew weaker. The diabetes, the heart condition, the neuropathy—the ailments—continued. The physical complications were enormous. We were in and out of hospitals. We spent time at the Mayo Clinic in Scottsdale. We consulted specialists of every sort. Waylon had to use a wheelchair to travel any real distance. At one point one foot had to be amputated at the ankle.

Amazingly, inspiringly, he accepted this deterioration without a trace of rancor. His inner strength was still mighty.

Jokingly, he'd say things like, "Looks like they're finally cutting me down to size."

I marveled how in his present condition this larger-than-life giant of a man could still laugh at himself, still find the energy to express love to all those who comforted him, still caress his guitar, still sing songs.

He had dreams but not nightmares. Some of those dreams, he said, were beautiful. A friend referred me to Hamlet's famous soliloquy where he reflects:

> *To die, to sleep.*
> *To sleep, perchance to dream; aye, there's the rub,*
> *For in that sleep of death what dreams may come*
> *When we have shuffled off this mortal coil,*
> *Must give us pause.*[2]

In his final months, Waylon did pause. Fully aware that he was facing his mortality, he looked death squarely in the face and did not blink. If anything, he became more curious, more openhearted.

During the Thanksgiving holiday of 2001, I took him to the hospital for still more procedures, none of which helped stem the downward spiral.

My heart told me that this was the moment he was ready to accept the Lord. But my heart had told me that before, and I had moved too quickly. Because my zeal had overwhelmed my sensitivity in the past, I didn't want to make the same mistake again. And yet my heart was insistent. My heart said, "Now is the time. Speak your truth."

As I looked at Waylon in the hospital bed, my heart was pounding.

"Looks like you want to say something to me, darlin'," he observed. "If you've got something to say, go ahead and say it."

Waylon sensed what was happening. He always did.

I took a deep breath and said the words. "Are you ready to accept the Lord?"

Waylon smiled. "I knew you were gonna ask that."

"It's a simple question," I said. "It all comes down to one thing, Waylon. Are you ready to be God's man?"

He nodded his head and kept repeating the phrase, "God's man, God's man."

"And to become God's man, what are the words I need to say?" Waylon asked.

"The words are that you accept him, that you love him as he loves you, that you turn your life over to him."

Waylon said those words. And when he did, I thought of the two words expressed in John 11:35: "Jesus wept."

I wept.

Waylon smiled.

He called me over to his bedside, took my hand, and said, "I love you so much."

He had declared his love for me a million times before, but this time his tone was so vulnerable, so soft, so sweet. He spoke with a sincerity that thrilled my heart. He spoke not only as my husband but, for the first time, as my brother in Christ.

Later that day Dulcie called to speak with him. During the course of their conversation, she asked Waylon to speak his confession of

Christ, and he did so without hesitation. His commitment to God was absolute.

The Christmas season was upon us. Valiantly, Waylon pressed on. He rested during the days and asked that I drive him through the desert at night. He simply wanted to see the stars and breathe the air. He wasn't boisterous but he wasn't gloomy. He spoke about his past, his parents, his childhood in Littlefield, his early infatuation with music. His children came to visit him. His friends rallied around. He'd ask me to sing the church hymns I had learned as a little girl. He and Coach talked about sports. He and Dulcie discussed the Lamb of God.

"I'm feeling confident," he said on New Year's Day 2002. "My body might be deserting me, but my soul is sound."

I loved hearing the word *confident*.

Despite the oxygen masks and tanks and the sundry medical apparatuses that would seem to destroy all confidence, his confidence remained intact. It was a new confidence, though—not the confidence of a superstar about to run up onstage to the cheers of a hundred thousand fans, but the quiet confidence of someone now calling himself "God's man."

February 13 was an ordinary day.

Coach and Waylon had plans to watch the Winter Olympics. I had plans to visit the chiropractor. After my appointment, I hurried home to make Waylon his daily treat, a big protein shake. When I arrived, Waylon was asleep—or at least appeared to be. But when I went to kiss his forehead, I detected no breath. I called to Coach, who was in the next room. He ran in and gave Waylon CPR. It was too late. Waylon had already made his transition. He had slipped into the other side of time.

The paramedics arrived and asked me to leave. I refused. I stayed and prayed in the Spirit: "God, this is your time. Whatever you decree, I accept. I know you can raise him up. If that's the testimony you want from me, I'll give it. But if you have already sent angels to receive him, amen. Your will be done."

I gave thanks to God Almighty for Waylon and for our time together.

I gave thanks to God for his salvation.

I gave thanks to God for his grace.

For his love.

For the blessing of this life.

And for life eternal.

Chapter 30

OUT OF THE ASHES

IT TOOK A LONG TIME TO RECOVER—A LONG, LONG TIME.

I was exhausted. I was numb. I hadn't realized the amount of energy I had devoted to Waylon's care. I hadn't considered the amount of anxiety I had been dealing with. Emotionally, I was drained.

Minister Will Campbell presided at the small service held at the mortuary. Connie Smith sang "Amazing Grace." I sang "Storms Never Last." Brother Will praised God for every good thing.

According to Waylon's wishes, we buried him in the Mesa cemetery near the graves of my mother and father. The tombstone, adorned with a picture of a smiling Waylon and his flying "W" logo, read:

WAYLON JENNINGS
JUNE 15, 1937–FEBRUARY 13, 2002
I AM MY BELOVED'S
MY BELOVED IS MINE.
A LOVING SON, HUSBAND, FATHER, AND GRANDFATHER.
A VAGABOND DREAMER,
A RHYMER AND SINGER OF SONGS.
A REVOLUTIONARY IN COUNTRY MUSIC

Later that day, I returned to the graveside. I wanted to be alone with Waylon. When I arrived, though, I saw that I would not be alone. An old man was standing in front of the tombstone. He was holding a stack of Waylon's albums in his arms. He had placed a boombox on the ground that was playing Waylon's greatest hits, "Honky Tonk Heroes," "I Ain't Living Long Like This," and "Lonesome, On'ry and Mean." His eyes were filled with tears as he placed the LPs on the grave.

When he turned and noticed me, he didn't register surprise. It was as though he expected me.

He said, "When I got back from Vietnam, he helped me. When I got divorced, he helped me. He helped me when I lost my job and he helped me when I lost my oldest son. He's always helped me."

"And he always will," I said, as I took the man's hand and stood there while Waylon sang "Women Do Know How to Carry On."

I did carry on. In March, with strong support from Shooter, I organized a memorial concert at the Ryman Auditorium in Nashville. We called it "I've Always Been Crazy: A Celebration of the Life and Legacy of Waylon Jennings." Our good friend, disc jockey Carl Mayfield, was the emcee. Shooter opened the show with his father's favorite, "I've Always Been Crazy." Kris Kristofferson sang "I Do Believe." Charley Pride sang "Good Hearted Woman." Hank Jr. sang his own "Eyes of Waylon."

Tributes poured in from everyone—from Neil Diamond to Kid Rock. Brother Will Campbell delivered a heartfelt eulogy, saying, "Waylon was a renegade, an outlaw, a man of faith, and a man of music. He was ministering all these years, and his ministries go on. We bid him godspeed with the words of another bard, 'Good night, sweet prince, and flights of angels sing thee to thy rest.'"

With the memorial service behind me, I returned to Arizona and ultimately settled on a comfortable ranchette on the Sonoran Desert north of Scottsdale. Thanks to Waylon's foresight and the specificity of his will, I had no financial stress.

In the beginning, I found the company of other widows critically important. I needed to hear their stories of grief and loss. I needed to learn their strategies for emotional survival. I needed role models to show me the way forward.

My family invited me on a fly fishing trip, but I declined. I didn't want to miss my weekly visits to Waylon's grave where I placed fresh flowers. I didn't want to leave. I didn't want to do anything. But fortunately my family wouldn't take no for an answer, and I found myself at Lees Ferry in Glen Canyon, just below the Arizona-Utah border at the base of the Colorado River, not far from the Grand Canyon. The setting overwhelmed me: the copper slate rocks, the blue-green river, the clean crisp air. I found healing in nature, though the healing of my heart remained a slow, slow process.

For the first time in my adult life, I was living alone. After all, I was nineteen when I married Duane and twenty-six when I married Waylon. I had no familiarity with a solitary life. And although I saw myself as a singer and songwriter, I had primarily seen myself as a wife and mother. Now that both my children, Jennifer and Shooter, were grown and on their own, and now that Waylon was gone, where did that leave me? Without Waylon to care for—to fret over, to pray over, to cherish and love—where would I direct my energy? I felt that half of me had died while half of me had lived.

I turned to prayer for solace. And, as always, prayer helped. I read and reread the Psalms, hearing an ancient musicality in the poetry of praise. Another sort of music helped enormously—the songs and singing of Ben Harper. I heard his *Will to Live* album, with songs like "Widow of a Living Man" and "I Shall Not Walk Alone," as a clarion call. I heard Ben calling me back to make music of my own.

From that call came *Out of the Ashes*, the album that marked my return as a recording artist. Don Was, the most sensitive of producers, said at the outset, "I want the majority of the cuts to be your original songs. I want this record to reflect the true you—what you're thinking and what you're feeling."

I had old songs and I had new songs. Songs are always rattling around my head, but I knew I had to start out prayerfully. So I began with "His Eye Is on the Sparrow." I also knew I wanted to feel comfortable in the studio. What a remarkable pleasure it was to reconnect with Jim Horn, the saxophonist who had played on my early singles when we were both teenagers! Waylon's longtime drummer Richie Albright made the date along with master musicians like guitarist Reggie Young and his cellist wife, our dear friend Jenny Lynn Hollowell. I worked especially closely with Ray Herndon, a great picker and vocalist with whom I wrote "You Can Pick 'Em," a song that sounded like a throwback to those early days when I was spitting out songs to help me deal with Waylon.

> There was the one from Memphis
> There was that one from West LA
> But the one from New Orleans
> She tried to put you in your grave
>
> There was the one from Texas
> Lord, she made you squirm
> But the one from Arizona
> Left you no soul at all
>
> You can pick 'em, baby
> But you know it's against the law

Imagery for another song, "The Phoenix Rises," came from my trip to Lees Ferry.

> New beginnings are so hard to find
> New beginnings are mountains to climb
> Blue sky over the horizon

But the sheer cliffs of copper pierce my mind
Emerald-green rivers speak quietly
And the black nights bring stars in my eyes

Outta the ashes, the Phoenix rises

I found a track of a song by Tony Joe White that had both Tony Joe
and Waylon's voices on it. I added my own as well as the stirring choir
of the Greater Apostolic Christ Temple. The theme fit perfectly: "Out
of the Rain."

I created love scenarios that both did and did not reflect my present state of mind. I called one "Never Got Over You."

These empty arms of desire, baby
Stayed open way too long
But I feel like I'm goin' crazy
But my love rages on

I'm not sure you've gotta heart, baby
Never seen love you make
You didn't think I'd go there
But you lead me all the way

I will never get over you

Other songs expressed my renewed desire for a romantic connection and what I termed "So Many Things":

So many things stand between us
Your heart and mine have touched this time
Our eyes can see us

Some bright blue autumn morning
Some wintery moonlight night
You'll reach for me and I'll come

Touch me, hold me like you do

Shooter's musical career had really begun to soar. Now, for the first time, we wrote a song together and sang it as a duet. It was important that it come as the record's last cut because, in the final analysis, "Please Carry Me Home" is a prayer.

When the bloodcurdlin' scream of the fear in my veins
Pierces the darkness circlin' my brain
When the pain in my soul is too great to explain
I reach out for you, I'm callin' Your name

Lord, please have mercy on my troubled soul
You keep me together when there's nothing to hold
Lord, please have mercy, I've nowhere to go
When the temptation is over, please carry me home

Out of the Ashes, released in 2006, was warmly received by critics and fans. It was cathartic, a release from my pent-up pain and a declaration of my status, both old and new, as a working artist.

I was back. And it was music that helped bring me back. Today my passion for music is as strong as ever. I especially love the bold and ever-changing music made by my son, Shooter. A few years back he released the brilliant *Waylon Forever*, a reshaping of the tracks that Shooter, at age sixteen, had cut with Waylon in 1995. With his band—the .357s—Shooter gave these old songs new and ingenious vitality. I am equally proud of my daughter Jennifer's musical talent, both as a gifted singer and as a skilled writer.

In 2014 I put out another record, *Live from Cain's Ballroom*, documenting a show I put on in Tulsa. The promoters billed me as "The First Lady of Outlaw Country"—a rubric that may not be all that accurate, but I'll take it for whatever it's worth. I had a ball that night and was especially delighted when Shooter came up and joined me on "Out of the Rain" and "Please Carry Me Home."

In 2016 I was delighted to appear on a televised tribute to Waylon and sing "Storms Never Last" with Kris Kristofferson. In turn, it was a double delight to honor Kris at his big tribute show in 2016 at the Bridgestone Arena in Nashville, where I was privileged to interpret one of his greatest compositions, "The Captive."

My most recent musical adventure involves the Psalms. Working with Lenny Kaye, Patti Smith's longtime guitarist and cowriter of Waylon's memoirs, I have approached these consecrated texts, these songs of David, with great reverence and respect. We have put them in a musical setting that, I pray, retains all their divine power. There is little ornamentation. My aim is to allow these blessed songs of praise to cry out now, as they have cried out for centuries, even as I first heard their faithful cry in my mother's church. The record will soon be released by Sony, and my dream is to travel to Israel, stay at the King David Hotel, and perform them in a sacred venue in the holy city of Jerusalem.

I've also been blessed to have worked diligently for a great many charities dealing with everything from music education for underprivileged children to research for pancreatic cancer.

———— ᙡ ————

Do I, some fifteen years after Waylon's passing, yearn for romance myself? I do. Even as I cherish my independence and am proud of the fact that I've learned to live alone, I'd like to share my life with a man. But I'm not a casual dater. When it comes to relationships, I have no interest in superficial connections. I'm looking for a serious friendship and a faithful commitment bonded by spirit. Early on, I came to see that a widow is an especially vulnerable creature. But blessedly, I've been protected by the Lord whose strength is my salvation.

Waylon, of course, continues to cast a long shadow over any potential romantic relationhip I might have with another man. His presence is everywhere in my home. His presence continues to comfort me. But, in seeking a new love, I am not looking to repeat the love I shared with Waylon. That was a love both great and unique. Even in retrospect, it brings me joy. A new love will look much different. I look forward to greeting that love with gratitude, knowing that, as always, God will provide the spiritual sustenance that makes this earthly journey an ongoing adventure.

Finally, I want to thank the living God of love for the infinite wonder of human life and the inexhaustible flow of creative energy that has allowed this story to be told.

Let the last words, from Psalm 91 (KJV), be his:

> *Because he hath set his love upon me,*
> *therefore will I deliver him:*
> *I will set him on high, because he hath known my name.*

ACKNOWLEDGMENTS

Jessi acknowledges:

My mother, who by her example taught me to believe, and my father, who, quiet and strong, never gave up.

Elsie P. Hand, for giving to Georgia and America her political guidance in education and banking—and for guiding me through widowhood.

Maureen Rafferty, who served our family and business faithfully—and also helped with this book's research and library of photos.

My musical family, who have kept me strong and encouraged—Reggie and Jenny Lynn Young; Carter and Barny Robertson; Robby Turner and Richie Albright—always there for me.

My girlfriends Addie Scavone and Lisa Kristofferson, true angels.

Nikki Mitchell and Terrie Lawrence, both poets and sisters, who encouraged me with my story.

My brother John Johnson, who remains the steel of our family, always there with spiritual guidance and practical assistance.

Cindy Denham, our accountant who always told us the truth.

Mike Vadin, tax attorney and friend.

My children and Waylon's children, all growing into fine human beings and carrying our lives forward.

David Ritz and Webster Younce, for confidence in my story.

Billy Mitchell, our lifetime photographer; Charles Gabrean, most recent photos taken in Arizona.

Don Kunz, our lawyer in Arizona, who won two very important court cases that affected our lives long-term, and his wife, Edith, my mentor for fashion, wit, and humor. They are lifetime friends.

Jay Goldberg, lawyer and jury consultant who oversaw and won Waylon's notorious "drug bust" case in Nashville. Jay and his wife, Rema, are family friends forever.

And of course all glory to God, my reason for living.

DAVID RITZ ACKNOWLEDGES:

Jessi, for a beautiful collaboration and meaningful friendship.

Webster Younce, for sensitive editing.

David Vigliano, for superb agenting.

Mark Rothbaum, for introducing me to Jessi.

And my beautiful wife, Roberta, my children, my grandchildren, and my friends, for all the loving support.

Thank you, Jesus.

Permissions for use of song lyrics:

"Never Got Over You" (Jessi Colter/Ray Herndon) © 2006 Higher Flame Publishing (BMI)/Yarman Songs (ASCAP); "Please Carry Me Home" (Jessi Colter/Shooter Jennings) © 2006 Higher Flame Publishing (BMI)/Faster and Harder Music/Universal Music Corp. (BMI); "So Many Things" (Jessi Colter) © 2006 Higher Flame Publishing (BMI); "The Phoenix Rises" (Jessi Colter) © 2006 Higher Flame Publishing (BMI); "You Can Pick 'Em" (Jessi Colter/Ray Herndon) © 2006 Higher Flame Publishing (BMI)/Yarman Songs (ASCAP); "God If I Could Only Write Your Love Song," written by Jessi Colter, © 1977 Helen D. Johnson Music (BMI), administered by Words & Music, a division of Big Deal Music, LLC. All Rights Reserved. Used by Permission. International Copyright Secured. "New Wine (From Heaven)," written by Jessi Colter, © 1977 Helen D. Johnson Music (BMI), administered by Words & Music, a division of Big Deal Music, LLC. All Rights Reserved. Used by Permission. International Copyright Secured. "Let It Go," written by Jessi Colter, © 1977 Helen D.

ACKNOWLEDGMENTS

Johnson Music (BMI), administered by Words & Music, a division of Big Deal Music, LLC. All Rights Reserved. Used by Permission. International Copyright Secured. "Put Your Arms Around Me," written by Jessi Colter, © 1977 Helen D. Johnson Music (BMI), administered by Words & Music, a division of Big Deal Music, LLC. All Rights Reserved. Used by Permission. International Copyright Secured. "There Ain't No Rain," written by Jessi Colter, © 1977 Helen D. Johnson Music (BMI), administered by Words & Music, a division of Big Deal Music, LLC. All Rights Reserved. Used by Permission. International Copyright Secured. "For Mama (AKA My Mama)," written by Jessi Colter, © 1977 Helen D. Johnson Music (BMI), administered by Words & Music, a division of Big Deal Music, LLC. All Rights Reserved. Used by Permission. International Copyright Secured. "I Belong To Him," written by Jessi Colter, © 1977 Helen D. Johnson Music (BMI), administered by Words & Music, a division of Big Deal Music, LLC. All Rights Reserved. Used by Permission. International Copyright Secured. "Master, Master," written by Jessi Colter, © 1977 Helen D. Johnson Music (BMI), administered by Words & Music, a division of Big Deal Music, LLC. All Rights Reserved. Used by Permission. International Copyright Secured. "Consider Me," written by Jessi Colter, © 1977 Helen D. Johnson Music (BMI), administered by Words & Music, a division of Big Deal Music, LLC. All Rights Reserved. Used by Permission. International Copyright Secured. "If She's Where You Like Livin' (You Won't Feel At Home With Me)," words and music by Jessi Colter, copyright (c) 1969 Universal-Songs of Polygram International, Inc. Copyright renewed. All rights reserved. Used by permission. *Reprinted by permission of Hal Leonard LLC;* "I Ain't The One," words and music by Jessi Colter, copyright (c) 1969 Universal-Songs of Polygram International, Inc. Copyright renewed. All rights reserved. Used by permission. *Reprinted by permission of Hal Leonard LLC;* "Don't Let Him Go," words and music by Jessi Colter, copyright (c) 1969 Universal-Songs of Polygram International, Inc. Copyright renewed. All rights reserved. Used by permission. *Reprinted by permission of Hal Leonard LLC;* "It's All Over Now," words and music by Jessi Colter, copyright (c) 1969 Universal-Songs of Polygram International, Inc. Copyright renewed. All rights reserved. Used by permission. *Reprinted by permission of Hal Leonard LLC;* "It's Morning (And I Still Love You)," words and music by Jessi Colter, copyright (c) 1975 Universal-Songs of Polygram International, Inc. Copyright renewed. All rights reserved. Used by permission. *Reprinted by permission of Hal Leonard LLC;* "Here I Am," words and music by Jessi Colter, copyright (c) 1975 Universal-Songs of Polygram International, Inc. Copyright renewed. All rights reserved. Used by permission. *Reprinted by permission of Hal Leonard LLC;* "Would You Leave Now," words and music by Jessi Colter, copyright (c) 1976 Universal-Songs of Polygram International, Inc. Copyright renewed. All rights reserved. Used by permission. *Reprinted by permission of Hal Leonard LLC;* "Rounder, Words and Music by Jessi Colter Copyright (c) 1975 Universal-Songs of Polygram International, Inc. Copyright renewed. All rights reserved. Used by permission. *Reprinted by permission of Hal Leonard LLC;* "Storms Never Last," words and music by Jessi Colter, copyright (c) 1975 Universal-Songs of Polygram International, Inc. Copyright renewed. All rights reserved. Used by permission. *Reprinted by permission of Hal Leonard LLC;* "What's Happened To Blue Eyes," words and music by Jessi Colter, copyright (c) 1975 Universal-Songs of Polygram International, Inc. Copyright renewed. All rights reserved. Used by permission. *Reprinted by permission of Hal Leonard LLC;* "I'm Not Lisa," words and music by Jessi Colter, copyright (c) 1972 Universal-Songs of Polygram International, Inc. Copyright renewed. All rights reserved. Used by permission. *Reprinted by permission of Hal Leonard LLC;* "Is There Any Way (You'd Stay Forever)," words and music by Jessi Colter, copyright (c) 1975 Universal-Songs of Polygram International, Inc. Copyright renewed. All rights reserved. Used by permission. *Reprinted by permission of Hal Leonard LLC;* "Let The Hand That Rocks The Cradle (Lead The Song)," words and music by Jessi Colter, copyright (c) 1975 Universal-Songs of Polygram International, Inc. Copyright renewed. All rights reserved. Used by permission. *Reprinted by permission of Hal Leonard LLC;* "I'm Living Proof (There's Life After You)," words and music by Roger Murrah and Waylon Jennings, copyright (c) 1987 Sony/ATV Music Publishing LLC and Waylon Jennings Music. All rights on behalf of Sony/ATV Music Publishing LLC administered by Sony/ATV Music Publishing LLC, 424 Church Street, Suite 1200, Nashville, TN 37219. International copyright secured. All rights reserved. *Reprinted by permission of Hal Leonard LLC.* "Please Carry Me Home," words and music by Jessi Colter and Shooter Jennings, copyright (c) 2004 Universal Music Corp., Faster N Harder Music and Higher Flame Music. All rights for Faster N Harder Music administered by Universal Music Corp. All rights reserved. Used by permission. *Reprinted by permission of Hal Leonard LLC;* "Darlin' It's Yours," words and music by Jessi Colter, copyright (c) 1976 Universal-Songs of Polygram International, Inc. Copyright renewed. All rights reserved. Used by permission. *Reprinted by Permission of Hal Leonard LLC;* "Oh, Will (Who Made It Rain Last Night)," words and music by Jessi Colter, copyright (c) 1976 Universal-Songs of Polygram International, Inc. Copyright renewed. All rights reserved. Used by permission. *Reprinted by Permission of Hal Leonard LLC;* "Angels Love Bad Men," words and music by Roger Murrah and Waylon Jennings, copyright (c) 1987 Sony/ATV Music Publishing LLC and Waylon Jennings Music. All rights on behalf of Sony/ATV Music Publishing LLC administered by Sony/ATV Music Publishing LLC, 424 Church Street, Suite 1200, Nashville, TN 37219. International copyright secured. All rights reserved. *Reprinted by permission of Hal Leonard LLC;* "You Deserve The Stars In My Crown," words and music by Roger Murrah and Waylon Jennings, copyright (c) 1987 Sony/ATV Music Publishing LLC and Waylon Jennings Music. All Rights on behalf of Sony/ATV Music Publishing LLC administered by Sony/ATV Music Publishing LLC, 424 Church Street, Suite 1200, Nashville, TN 37219. International copyright secured. All rights reserved. *Reprinted by permission of Hal Leonard LLC;* "You Hung The Moon (Didn't You Waylon?)," words and music by Jessi Colter, copyright (c) 1976 Universal-Songs of Polygram International, Inc. Copyright renewed. All rights reserved. Used by permission. *Reprinted by Permission of Hal Leonard LLC;* "Without You," words and music by Jessi Colter, copyright (c) 1969 Universal-Songs of Polygram International, Inc. Copyright renewed. All rights reserved. Used by permission. *Reprinted by Permission of Hal Leonard LLC.*

NOTES

Chapter 1: Arizona at Night

1. Sara Teasdale, "Night in Arizona," http://www.theotherpages.org/poems/teasd01.html, public domain.

Chapter 2: When Time and Eternity Meet

1. C. S. Lewis, *The Screwtape Letters* (New York: HarperCollins, 2009), 81.
2. "When Time and Eternity Meet," traditional hymn, public domain.

Chapter 3: Beyond the Mountains of the Moon

1. Edgar Allan Poe, "Eldorado" (1903), *The Works of Edgar Allan Poe*, Lit2Go Edition, accessed July 25, 2016, http://etc.usf.edu/lit2go/147/the-works-of-edgar-allan-poe/5283/eldorado/, public domain.

Chapter 11: Rhythms

1. Waylon Jennings and Lanny Kaye, *Waylon: An Autobiography* (Chicago: Chicago Review Press, 2012), 112.

Chapter 22: Flying High, Falling Low

1. Thomas Merton, *The Seven Storey Mountain, Fiftieth Anniversary Edition* (New York: Harcourt, 1998), 248.

Chapter 23: Patience

1. *Waylon*, 287.
2. Ibid., 291.

NOTES

CHAPTER 25: UNEXPECTED BIRTH
1. *Waylon.*

CHAPTER 29: THIS MORTAL COIL
1. "Will the Circle Be Unbroken?" is a popular Christian hymn written in 1907 by Ada R. Habershon with music by Charles H. Gabriel. Public domain.
2. William Shakespeare, *Hamlet*, act 3, scene 1.

ABOUT THE AUTHORS

JESSI COLTER IS ONE OF AMERICA'S MOST BELOVED SINGER-songwriters. Her storied career began in the sixties when, encouraged by her first husband, guitar legend Duane Eddy, she composed hit songs for Dottie West, Nancy Sinatra, and Hank Locklin. Best known for her collaboration with her husband Waylon Jennings and for her 1975 country-pop crossover hit "I'm Not Lisa," she was the only woman featured on the landmark album *Wanted: The Outlaws* that forever changed American music. She has fifteen major-label albums to her credit, and her songs and records have sold in the tens of millions. She lives near Scottsdale, Arizona.

DAVID RITZ, CALLED "ONE OF THE MOST PROLIFIC AND RESPECTED music biographers of the modern era" by the *New York Times*, has collaborated with, among others, Willie Nelson, Ray Charles, Aretha Franklin, and B.B. King.

JESSI COLTER
THE PSALMS
The New Album
12 Powerful Original Recordings
With Lyrics Drawn From The Psalms
Produced by Lenny Kaye
Available Now
JESSI COLTER
THE PSALMS
LEGACY